Rural Urban Framework

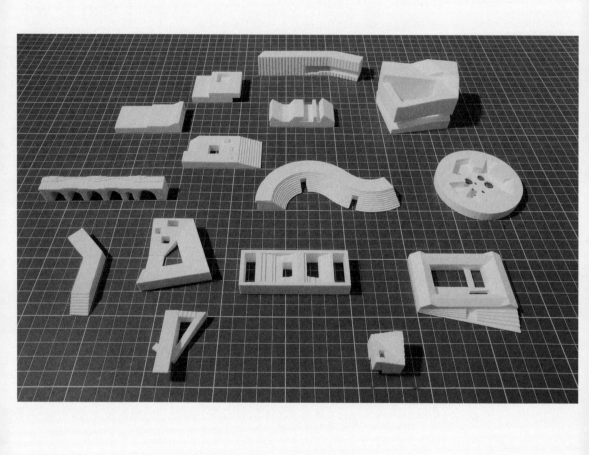

Rural Urban Framework

TRANSFORMING
THE CHINESE COUNTRYSIDE

Joshua Bolchover
& John Lin

Birkhäuser
Basel

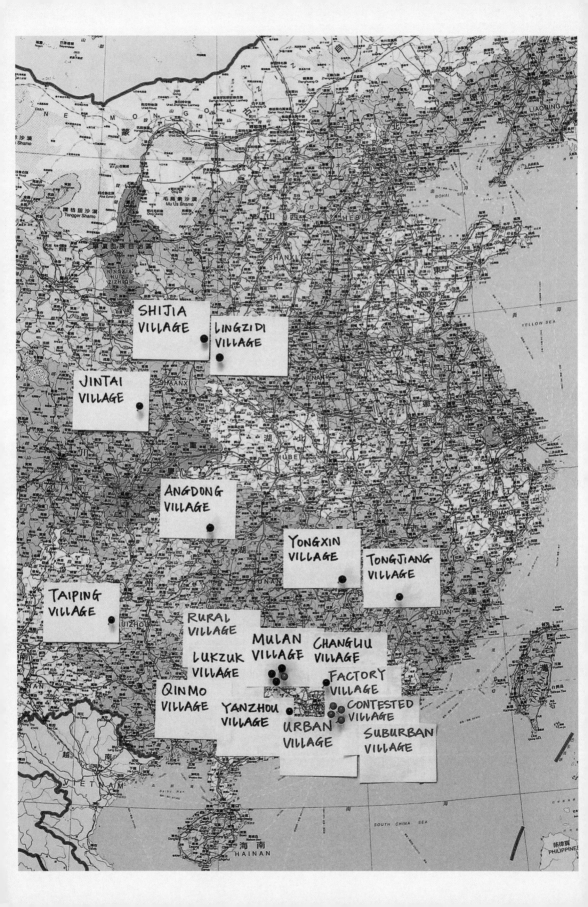

TABLE OF CONTENTS

A Hong Kong
B Qinmo Village

Research and Design in China

THE JOURNEY
Research and Design in China

Rural Urban Framework began as a journey to a project site in a rural village near the border of Guangdong and Guanxi Province in 2006. The eight-hour drive started in Hong Kong, travelled across the border to Shenzhen, and commenced northward up through the Pearl River Delta. The journey took us through a cross-section of distinct urban concentrations and indeterminate amalgamations of built fabric and farmland, before arrival at our rural destination. The journey revealed a landscape that was in a state of incompletion and transition. We began to document this territory observing collisions, paradoxes, abandonment, synergies, and contestation. Given that nearly all of the land that we passed through had been farmland thirty years ago, we began to categorize each of these conditions and to investigate the distinct processes underlying their formation. As our work takes us across China to various other remote locations, we remain interested not only in the diversity of project sites but in the journey from the city to the countryside and in the transformation of rural to urban fabric.

As a result of this journey, we established Rural Urban Framework as a research and design collaborative. Established as a non-profit organization within the University of Hong Kong, we engage with charities and government organizations to design projects in China. By engaging the context through design, the aim is to research the processes of rural urbanization.

This book explores the fate of over eighteen rural villages. Some have become embedded in dense urban fabric with few traces of their agricultural origins remaining, others have had their farmland turned into residential enclaves, and some have been fragmented, as the forces of urbanization encroached upon their rural livelihoods. The book itself is organized as a journey: with case-study villages beginning in urban areas, transgressing through various states before reaching rural village sites. The scales of the projects vary, from small interventions that address large scale forces to designing and planning entire villages. Each architectural project responds to the unique conditions posited by each village location. Each addresses different themes and problematic issues engendered by the urbanization process. The projects are not one-stop solutions nor should they be heralded as altruistic archetypes. If anything they are experiments, designed to be robust enough to withstand and adapt to the rapidly changing context. Completed projects and failed projects are both presented here, as often un-built projects bring to light and clarify our understanding of the complex forces acting on these sites.

In many emergent, urbanizing areas of China, the once clear distinction between rural and urban has become obsolete in the face of processes that have blurred their definition. The Chinese context provides an ideal laboratory for understanding these new village conditions, given that they all originated from a single homogeneous type. In China and the world, we live in an urban age, but we believe its future course is intertwined with the fate of the rural.

↖ Map of the journey
   to Qinmo Village
   in 2006

↪ pp. 8/9: Photographs
   taken along the journey

↖ Plan panorama
showing the five village
conditions

RURAL URBAN FRAMEWORK
Village Urbanization

Thirty years ago the majority of people in China were farmers. They lived in simple village houses and owned land collectively. Today the radical transformation brought about through China's economic reforms has completely restructured this predominantly rural population in terms of their work, their leisure time, their homes, their incomes, their family structures, and their aspirations. This has produced a completely stratified society from the very rich to an emergent middle-class to people who have remained seemingly unchanged and still farm the land. This new societal structure has resulted in a new spatial logic whereby the binary relationship between rural and urban is no longer valid. Built form, density, and population levels that one would typically attribute to urban areas are still legally defined as rural land. The 20th-century relationship between the core and the periphery, the center and the suburbs has been superseded by a gradated blanket of urbanization. This is not sprawl in the conventional understanding, or the result of an exodus from urban centers to suburban belts such as has occurred in Western cities. Rather this process of urbanization is tied directly to its origins as rural land. In this sense the rural is an active agent in this evolving process of urban transformation.

One reason that the rural has had such a profound effect is due to the Hukou registration policy (instigated in the Mao era and still in use today) whereby every citizen is registered as either a rural or urban resident depending on where they were born. This policy distinguishes between land development rights, health care and access to education thereby regulating and enforcing the division between the city and the countryside. The land-use rights of rural citizens, enacted through village collectives, has meant that land is developed more rapidly and more speculatively than in urban areas, which are predominantly planned through the formal mechanisms of government.

As a result the inter-relation between urban processes and rural processes has produced a diverse landscape of blurred, ambiguous territories as land is being transformed. It is these zones that play out the contestation between policies, land ownership, development rights, and individual land speculation; between farmers, developers, local government, factory owners, or foreign investors. These zones represent a critical juncture in China's ongoing economic revival—they bring to light unresolved regulations or loopholes in the system, black-market grey areas and discrepancies between individual and collective action, between individual profit and compensation. They demonstrate specific forms of urbanization producing unique characteristics. They often describe in-between states: half finished, partially abandoned, or half demolished. To this extent they are dynamic, exemplifying the struggle between local and large scale forces attributable to global economic development.

In travelling through this landscape between the urban and rural, we have observed irrational and unpredictable adjacencies: fish ponds next to factories, abandoned houses next to new tower blocks, informal settlements next to formally planned commercial blocks, farmland next to golf courses. In researching the forces behind such spatially diverse terrains we have identified five different conditions: Urban Village, Factory Village, Suburban Village, Contested Village, and Rural Village. At the beginning they were all the same—they were all villages.

↓ Map of the Pearl
   River Delta indicating
   different conditions

■ Urban Village
■ Factory Village
■ Suburban Village
■ Contested Village
■ Farmland
■ Water

Urban Village

Urban villages are enclaves that have emerged as a direct result of the difference in policy over land-use rights between urban land and rural land. In developing cities such as Shenzhen, development forces come from both top down formal processes and via the mechanisms of rural villages. Entrepreneurial and speculative, the urban villages provide an alternate urban reality to that of the generic city, providing super dense migrant housing, black-market services such as prostitution and gambling, and often have distinct ethnic identities. As the generic formal city expands, the urban villages become islands of difference within a sea of similarity. In a certain way this mirrors the "One Country, Two Systems" policy that the Mainland government utilizes for irregular political and legal entities such as Hong Kong and Macao. Urban villages operate in a similar way within the construct of the city as "One City, Two Systems." They have evolved through differences in citizens rights, land development, political organization, housing types and economic exchange, yet the two systems—the formal and informal—are interlocked into a relationship of codependency whereby one is necessitated by the other.

Factory Village

Industrial production took hold after 1978 as global industries relocated to take advantage of the attractive conditions offered by the special economic zones, such as financial incentives, abundant resources of land and cheap labor. As a result many villages swapped fields for factories. In addition, a relaxation in regulations governing agricultural production allowed villagers to start up their own enterprises or build factories for lease. The scope and diversity of industries that these initiatives catalyzed is vast ranging: from small scale village entities, to inter-village networks producing singular products, to city-scale gated compounds containing 300,000 plus workers. For rapidly urbanizing cities, such as Dongguan, the city fabric is interspersed with numerous typologies of factory developments and workers' dormitories. Synergies exist between these factory compounds and the natural villages that surround them. Often workers go there in their free time or for better food; in many cases they choose to live in the village as a familiar setting compared to the designated dormitory blocks. The vast migration of rural migrants into these factory agglomerations has been facilitated by social and kinship networks that link back to their home villages. In turn, as factories generate wealth, the higher level managers and factory workers become part of a middle class seeking residential upgrades. The intermixing of factory compounds, village conditions, and housing developments creates a distinctive urban patchwork with each individual programmatic patch undergoing different stages in the industrial urbanization process.

Suburban Village

The middle class in China has yet to be defined. Pre-1978 everyone was considered to be equal. Since then, the economic restructuring has produced many wealthy people, some of whom used to be farmers. Some of these villagers have become rich by building houses for migrant workers, or by starting up their own businesses, or through renting land to developers and factories. The emergence of a stratified income sector of the population has led to a demand for lifestyle choice, in many respects to reinforce and represent this change in financial status for this aspirant group. This has resulted in the creation of suburban typologies such as golf real-estate developments, gated tower compounds, theme-parks, and shopping malls. Unlike the out-of-town model these developments exist within the urban development of the city. Designations of "good" versus "bad" districts are not yet the primary drivers of real estate speculation as found in many Western cities, yet these property islands are often demarcated, walled, and securely segregated from their surrounding urban context. As the numbers of the middle class increase in China, how this group of people decides to live will have a profound effect on the evolution of the city, dramatically impacting consumption patterns, energy usage, and economic growth.

Contested Village

In the process of rapid development, policy changes, and land reform, legal constructs have had to evolve to try to keep pace with new, unforeseen conditions. Their implementation by the vast network of governance from the provincial level down to the village can lead to misunderstandings or simply non-adherence. As a result black-market loopholes emerge, which become exploited for new development opportunities.
In particular the potential for corruption is rife as individuals or village collectives seek mechanisms to develop rural land into profitable investments. Contestations between numerous stakeholders including villagers, local governments, developers, and factory owners arise through the ambiguity of development rights, compensation, and the status of rural or urban land.
In some areas these conflicts have led to a stalemate or waiting game whereby villagers are holding out for better compensation resulting in fragmented sites intermixing farmland, abandoned construction plots, or new residential blocks.

Rural Village

At first glance the rural village seems unchanged by the events of the last thirty years. What becomes apparent is the contradiction between the construction of new family houses versus a seemingly dwindling population. The village contains predominantly the old and the young with anyone of working age having left to earn money in the cities. As these migrants work they send a large proportion of their income back to their remaining relatives in the village. The money is typically used to construct new, modern homes enabling the villagers to vacate their old, traditional houses. Partly serving as status symbols within the village, the size, number of floors, and materials used denote the economic success of the family. The poorest are the ones with no families who maintain their livelihood in the same manner as they did prior to the economic reforms. Meanwhile the farmland is used without any urge for efficiency of production, and crops are predominantly used for subsistence. The result is that the village has become economically dependent on the city, yet it still holds a symbolic and meaningful resonance as home.

Framework

These five categories describe a society and landscape undergoing radical transformation. The processes of urban change and their spatial products are unique and unprecedented in China. These conditions form the foundation of our work: to undertake research and to design projects. The research sets out to investigate the processes of transformation acting on our five transitory states through fieldwork, interviews, and time-based documentation. The objective of studying micro-conditions is to gain a further understanding of larger themes and issues associated with territorial urbanization in these sample sites. This context is the backdrop of our work as architects. Though each project site is unique, it can be categorized according to one of the five research themes. In each case we aim to respond to contextual issues that have surfaced through the research: for example, the reprogramming of an old school building into a demonstration farm as an attempt to insert a new economy into the village, so that villagers can become less reliant on remittances sent from their children. All of our projects resist the normative generic building typology so prevalent in China today. Instead, we seek to provide innovative and unique spaces that work within local constraints of budget, workmanship, materials, and construction methods. The relationship between research and projects is not one-to-one, yet our objective is to see them as parallel and codependent processes whereby each can inform the other. This is what we understand as a framework: a working methodology that sets up a productive dialogue between research and design in order to make architecture that actively contributes to the future transformation of the areas in which it is located.

↗ *Rural Urban Ecology* exhibited at the Venice Biennale, Hong Kong Pavilion in 2010. The panorama is a collage of over one hundred research photographs of the journey from urban to rural territory.

↖ Detail of a project
model as a viewing
device to the context
behind

Urban Village

ENCLAVE URBANISM

Urban villages, or villages-amid-the city, have emerged as unique forms of urban spaces in Chinese cities. The mechanisms of their transformation, rooted in their origins as rural villages, posit an interesting dynamic between top-down policy and its informal interpretation and enactment via individual actors, families, or village organizations. Their naming embodies a dialectical tension between the rural and the urban that is played out in the transformation of urban form and its functioning and differentiation from other parts of the city.

They exist as island enclaves, distinct through their physical form, the programs and activities that take place there, the concentration of migrants who live there, and the regulatory frameworks that they operate under. They go against the grain of formal city-building and planning in China, engendering and fostering a type of urbanity that contains a diversity of spatial conditions, entrepreneurial actions, and multiple stakeholders. As anomalies, they are threatened and many have been eradicated in favor of more sanitized and homogeneous urban forms that create a seamless cityscape without any awkward aberrations. Many city governments use the rhetoric of progress to argue that urban villages are unhygienic, unsafe, and are in desperate need of modernization, which echo many of the historical post-war slum clearance programs in the United Kingdom and the United States. However, if they are erased what would be lost in this process? How would their elimination affect the surrounding urban districts? Are there specific urban forms; building typologies, public spaces, or constellations of programs that are present in urban villages which could be harnessed in the future development of these locations? Do they contain urban design ideas that could be extracted and deployed to offer alternative solutions to the normative models of urban planning so prevalent in the construction of Chinese cities today?

* The indented text is written by Mary Ann O'Donnell, a social anthropologist based in Shenzhen who first introduced me to Tangtou in November 2012.

Literally these neighborhoods are called *cheng zhong cun*, or city-inside-villages. This ordering is important because Chinese naming practices go from largest to smallest territory. In other words, the Chinese emphasizes the fact that these neighborhoods are "out of place," while the English reminds us that the *cheng zhong cun* have a particular kind of independent agency and identity.*

By framing the question in terms of *cheng zhong cun* (城中村), influencing the city (rather than the city shaping the neighborhood), this article goes against the grain of Chinese territorial norms, even as it affirms critical practices in Western scholarship. The distinction between Chinese territorial practices and Western intellectual practices matters because it illustrates the extent to which Western descriptions of *cheng zhong cun* are not and cannot be value-neutral. The larger question for progressive scholarship thus becomes one of self-reflexivity: "To what ends have we activated this rupture?"

In order to answer these questions the essay will focus on Baishizhou, an urban village settlement in Shenzhen, Southern China. As Shenzhen became the first city in China to eliminate the legal status of all of its villages in 2004, it is at the forefront of testing whether this policy will facilitate the smooth incorporation of these villages back into the legal and physical construct of the city. However, this process is fraught with complexity that belies the implicit resistance of these villages-amid-the-city.

Residual Histories

Emerging from the Baishizhou subway stop one first encounters the six-lane highway of Shennan Road, Shenzhen's main East-West corridor. Across the street, tourist buses congregate and the tops of replicas of the Eiffel tower and a sandy pyramid can be seen behind the gates of Windows of the World, one of China's earliest theme-parks, which opened in 1994. Down the street a recently constructed mall, Yitian Holiday Plaza—"The Most Wonderful

↖ Urban village cluster, Shenzhen

→ Plan of Baishizhou urban village cluster within Shenzhen's urban context. The Mao era, Tangtou dormitories are highlighted in pink.

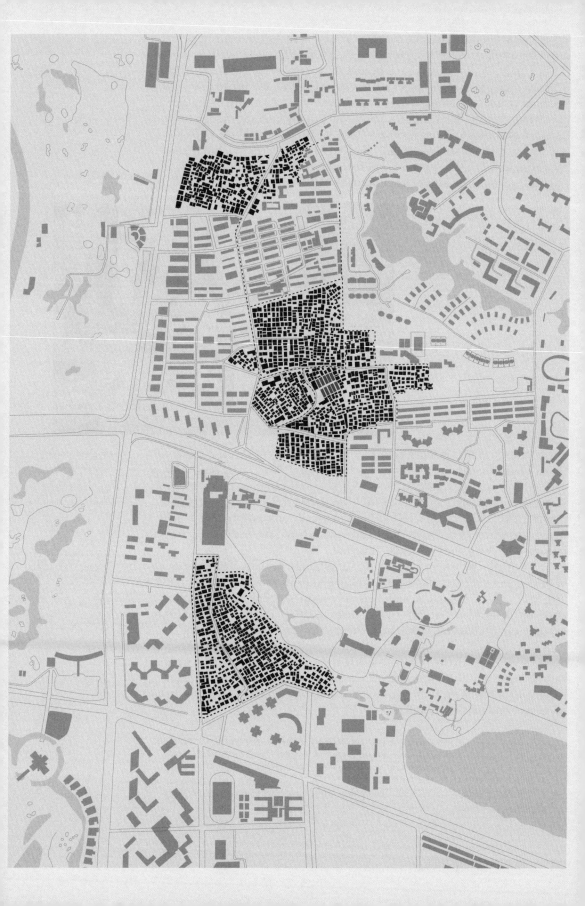

Experiential Shopping Mall in China"—contains all the prerequisites of contemporary urban living for China's new middle class: Starbucks, H&M, Cartier, an ice skating rink, a cinema, and an up-market Westin Hotel. Taking a Google Earth view of this piece of the city a very different urban morphology becomes visible. An amorphous spill of densely packed houses, irregularly organized, extends north-south on both sides of the highway hidden behind Shennan Road's middle class veneer. This cluster is Baishizhou, one of Shenzhen's last remaining centrally located urban villages and home to approximately 140,000 people—approximately the population of Oxford, England—living in an area of just 7.4 km².

↖ A typical street in Baishizhou

Baishizhou is in fact a conjugation of five villages. Three of these, (Baishizhou, Shangbaishi, Xianbaishi) are "natural," originally rural villages and two are "administrative" villages (Xintang and Tangtou) that were set up by the state during Mao's Great Leap Forward (1958–62). Today the boundaries of these villages are blurred and usually only visibly demarcated by a road or through different street address plaques. Spatial differences occur but are subtle with one exception—Tangtou.

Tangtou is distinct as it contains a residual fragment of its rural past in the form of five rows of one-stroy workers' dormitories that accommodate eighty-six households. These buildings were constructed in 1959 when the government decided that the original Tangtou village in Shiyan, about 15 km northwest of Baishizhou, was to be flooded to form a new reservoir. The residents were relocated to a newly set up agricultural work unit—the Shahe State Farm. Through this process the original Tangtou residents, who were rural villagers, became part of the state apparatus. This initial move was the origin for the latent ambiguity in status and ownership rights that underlaid all further evolution of the village.

This is a good example of how societal units are very clearly organized and defined in Chinese terms. In Chinese, the difference between a "cheng zhong village" and a "village" marks an important social boundary between historic identities and the unintended effects of urbanization in Shenzhen. In Mandarin usage "village" or "cun" usually refers to one self-identified group, while cheng zhong cun would refer to all of Baishizhou.

1   Dikötter, Frank. 2010. *Mao's Great Famine: The History of China's Most Devastating Catastrophe, 1958–62.* Bloomsbury Publishing, London, New York, Berlin and Sydney

During the periods of extreme volatility and hardship in the Mao era,[1] (Great Leap Forward, Cultural Revolution), many villagers within the county of Bao'an where Tangtou is located abandoned their homes and attempted to flee across the border to adjacent, British-ruled Hong Kong. To maintain agricultural production within Bao'an, the government installed work units, such as the Shahe State Farm, and used these to accommodate overseas Chinese who were being repatriated from countries undergoing political turmoil across Asia: for example, the violent communist suppression and killing of Chinese citizens in Suharto's Indonesia during 1965–66.

Bao'an remained an agricultural county composed of natural villages and state farms producing lychees, bananas, rice, and oysters up until Deng Xiaoping's radical economic reforms of 1979. Deng selected Bao'an as a laboratory for economic growth because of its adjacent border with Hong Kong and elevated it to the status of Shenzhen Municipality. The mechanism for growth was the apparatus of the Special Economic Zone (SEZ) that encouraged the influx of foreign investment through opportune regulatory conditions to stimulate industrial production. Initially incorporating the entire county of $1953\,km^2$, by 1981 it became apparent this was simply too large to manage and the area was split into Shenzhen Special Economic Zone

2   O'Donnell, Mary Ann. 2001. "Becoming Hong Kong, Razing Baoan, Preserving Xin'an: An Ethnographic Account of Urbanization in the Shenzhen Special Economic Zone." *Cultural Studies* Issue 3–4, Volume 15, pp. 419–443

$(327\,km^2)$ and New Bao'an County $(1626\,km^2)$.[2] Despite this re-designation in naming, land ownership was split between state-owned land and rural land. In 1982 the constitution clarified that rural land was owned by village collectives, urban land was owned by the state, and that land could be transferred to the state through the mechanism of expropriation whereby villagers would receive compensation to replace their income and their home. By 1983 the constitution allowed those citizens with rural hukou (the designation in the the registration system set up by Mao to distinguish between rural citizens and urban citizens) to migrate to cities to work as long as they maintained their original registration status and still kept up their agricultural quota. And in 1984 the constitution allowed villagers to diversify their activities on their own private plots, permitting them to build houses, and undertake industrial activities or commercial ventures as long as they had

3   Lin, George C. S., and Samuel P. S. Ho. 2005. "The State, Land System, and Land Development Processes in Contemporary China." *Annals of the Association of American Geographers*, Vol. 95, No. 2 (June 2005), pp. 411–436

been approved by the village collective.[3] These reforms impacted the SEZ dramatically. Many migrants came to work in the assembly factories or to work on construction sites as a result of the state implementing its first master plan in 1982. Local villagers responded to this new influx of population by building rental homes so the migrants had somewhere to live, or by opening shops and restaurants. The earliest houses built in the early 1980s were two-to three-story villas, however these were soon superseded by six-to ten-story urban blocks known as "handshake buildings" (握手樓, *woshou lou*, literally "kissing building" in Chinese), so called because of the ability to shake your neighbor's hand simply by reaching out of the window. The scale of these buildings made it likely that in order to finance the construction, villagers would probably have asked for investment from other sources: either as a joint venture with other villagers or from family members in Hong Kong, Taiwan, or other parts of China. This building typology has become the dominant type that characterizes urban villages throughout Shenzhen. The buildings are illegal structures in that they violate many building codes that Shenzhen subsequently implemented to regulate urban construction. Importantly, building codes have evolved with Shenzhen's urban boom and so the *cheng zhong cun* are not the only neighborhoods where building stock can be retrospectively considered as substandard. As early as 1986 the authorities attempted to regulate them through setting a maximum building height of three stories and maximum area of 40 m² per family member. However the threat of fines was an ineffective deterrent as the profit margin remained consistently seductive throughout the 1990s.

The handshake buildings create a dense urban mass separated by thin crevices of light. These crevices contain services for the buildings: drain pipes, electric wires, air-conditioning units, and drying racks for wet clothes. In some cases the gaps are so narrow that they often just become dumping sites for rubbish and waste. Those that are wide enough to walk down as alleyways create a secondary network of pedestrian flow from the single lane roads that carve through the urban blocks. Walking through one of the alleys in Tangtou one emerges into an urban clearing that reveals the one-story grid of the collective dormitories. The relative openness of this space and

↙ The public space used as night-market or basketball court

↓ The dormitory workers' houses from the Mao era

visibility of the sky contrasts with the claustrophobia of the handshakes. This space and the agricultural dormitories within it distinguish Tangtou from other urban villages. The grid consists of ten buildings distributed in a grid of five by two. The spaces between the blocks are used for storage, drying clothes, plants, or just chatting with your neighbor. Some of the buildings are in disrepair, windows are broken, roof tiles are missing, while others have been augmented with new extensions, awnings, and recently applied render. Adjacent to the blocks is a rectangular public space that, depending on the time of day, serves as a basketball court, a night market, and an expansion of the various restaurants that surround its edge. A well sits alongside this space and still provides water for washing, cleaning, and cooking. Without the circumscribing wall of handshake buildings, this cluster operates and looks like many other rural villages. It is not so hard to imagine that these buildings were once surrounded by farmland.

> Portable prefabricated dormitories for migrant workers on construction sites throughout Shenzhen reproduce the underlying design of the collective dormitories. Although made of steel rather than simple concrete and bricks, like the Tangtou collective dormitories, the prefabricated dormitories are single- or double-story buildings, consisting of narrow living areas with shared amenities, which are arranged in lines that create alleys and neighborhoods. Moreover, these buildings are constructed with an eye to a future in which they will be replaced. Importantly, this architectural similarity is a function of the intended residents of both Tangtou and construction site dormitories—migrant workers—who have (been) relocated to labor on state projects (such as Shenzhen's subway, for example). In other words, the collective dormitories, like the prefabricated steel dormitories, are the architectural vehicle through which farmers literally inhabited the Chinese state.

Palimpsest

The presence of different building typologies—the farm dormitories, the three-story houses, and the handshakes—each from different eras and policy directives, provide evidence of the different stages of transformation from rural to urban fabric. In this regard Baishizhou and Tangtou can be understood as palimpsests that are inscribed with these historical layers of change. While the handshake buildings reflect the evolution of the villagers from farmers to real estate developers and active agents in the production of urban form, the older fragment reflects the lingering ambiguity in status of the original Tangtou villagers.

In the government's view, the villagers had forgone their rural citizen rights by working on the state farm and had become, in effect, urban citizens. In the villagers view, they were still fundamentally operating as rural citizens; they were still farming the land; still retained their rural hukou; and although they didn't have official rural rights to the surrounding land, as did their natural-village counterparts, they nevertheless claimed and built on this land during the frenzied industrialization of the late 1980s and early 1990s.[4] The dormitory blocks were not developed since they were officially part of the Shahe collective farm and so administratively they were considered to be state-controlled land. This anomaly in development now provides Tangtou with its uniqueness—a residual historic fragment in a city that retains little and is in a constant state of change.

4 O'Donnell, Mary Ann. 1999. "Path Breaking: Constructing Gendered Nationalism in the Shenzhen Special Economic Zone." *Positions.* 7(2), pp. 343–375

As visceral evidence of the rural origins of the *cheng zhong cun*, the Tangtou dormitories disrupt complacent narratives about boomtowns and progress in the post Mao era. Under Mao, village dormitories represented the Chinese state's efforts to rebuild and strengthen rural communities. Moreover, peasants—along with workers and soldiers—were key figures in the revolutionary state. In contrast, contemporary prefabricated steel dormitories have been designed to vanish from public view, erasing traces of rural labor and the social conditions of this labor. Consequently, plans to raze and rebuild *cheng zhong cun* must also be understood against this larger effort to redescribe the Chinese nation as one without peasants.

Stagnation

Despite efforts to clamp down on illegal building and to control the development of the urban villages, construction continued throughout the 1990s. In 2005, to prove its seriousness of purpose, the government demolished eighteen, eight-story handshake buildings in the village of Futian Yunongcun.[5] Subsequently, a more inconspicuous policy has led to the urban villages reaching development stasis and a stagnation in the evolution of the palimpsest.

The villages-to-residents policy first introduced in 1992 to the inner district and in 2004 to the entire metropolitan area meant that rural villagers had their citizen status changed from rural to urban hukou and all village collectives were transformed into shareholder cooperatives. This meant that villagers owned their buildings but not the land that they were built on. Given that the majority of these buildings breached regulations and were in fact deemed illegal, should a resident decide to knock the building down and attempt to build anew, it would allow the government, through the resident committee, to reclaim the land and control development much more stringently. This deterrent was effective as villagers had no choice: in order to preserve their investment in their buildings it was simply best to leave things as they were and wait until they were approached with a substantial compensation package.

> Traditionally, Southern Chinese villages were defined through lineages (father to son or "same surname") and land. In other words, village membership meant more than simply doing agricultural labor, it entailed having land rights through membership in a corporate group. The villages-to-residents policy redefined village holdings in terms of buildings rather than land. Importantly, this policy did not dissolve the corporate links between villagers, traditional institutions that often had histories of more than 400 years and that had been strengthened through modern bureaucracy when these villages were incorporated into the Chinese state apparatus as "work teams" and "work brigades." For example, during the Mao era, Tangtou was a work team. In the post Mao era, it reverted to the traditional name of "village." However, this shift in nomenclature did not mean that the villages ceased to use modern bureaucracy to organize themselves. Instead, the "villages" re-activated traditional identities in the context of an already existing bureaucratic institutional structure. Thus another implied meaning of the expression *cheng zhong cun* includes this disjuncture between identification with the institutional structures of the recently established city and continued identification with one's restructured village.[6]

This compensation package has to provide for the income generated through the land-use rights and for the building based on an area rate. The amount is negotiated by the developers, rather than the government, who negotiate with the resident committee, who in turn, negotiate with individual villagers.

5 Bach, Jonathan. 2010. "They Come in Peasants and Leave Citizens': Urban Villages and the Making of Shenzhen, China." *Cultural Anthropology*. Vol. 25, Issue 3, pp. 421–458

6 O'Donnell, Mary Ann. 2008. "Vexed Foundations: An Ethnographic Interpretation of the Shenzhen Built Environment." Paper presented at *Vexed Urbanism: A Symposium on Design and the Social*, The New School, New York, Feb 13–15

Consequently taking ownership of land in urban villages for redevelopment is complex. Each building consists of multiple stakeholders with multiple investments. For example, one family might manage several flats within several buildings, have a commercial unit in another, and be leasing land rights somewhere else. In the case of Baishizhou any large scale development plan would also have to be undertaken with the agreement of five different village committees.

In effect the only mode of evolution of the village, or any urban village, is through large-scale redevelopment as determined by government master plans and facilitated by premier development companies. This has two effects. Firstly, this has led to stagnation in the development process and the gradual demise of the existing buildings within the village. Incremental development is not possible and so buildings can be only partially augmented or repaired at best. This stymies entrepreneurial development from alternative sets of stakeholders either via individuals, collectives, or family networks. It closes down options for financial opportunism leaving the negotiation for compensation packages as the last step in the transformation process from rural to urban land. Additionally, through insisting that the village be developed in its entirety with the burden for compensation being placed on the developer, the scale of the investment becomes very high. In order to recoup such significant expenditure most developers resort to large scale high-rise podium tower blocks designed for an upwardly mobile, new middle class.

→ Augmented roof structure

↘ Tangle of electric cables serving village buildings

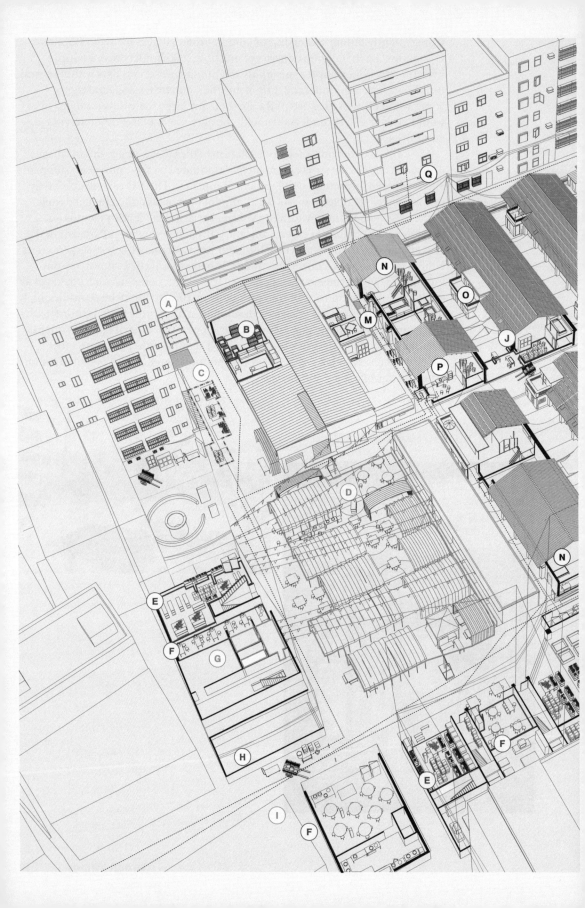

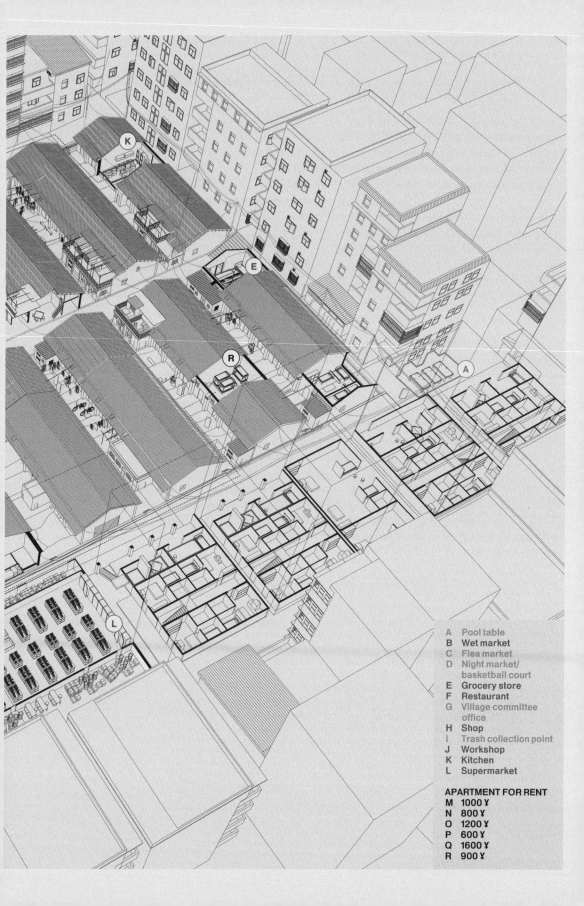

A   Pool table
B   Wet market
C   Flea market
D   Night market/
     basketball court
E   Grocery store
F   Restaurant
G   Village committee
     office
H   Shop
I   Trash collection point
J   Workshop
K   Kitchen
L   Supermarket

APARTMENT FOR RENT
M   1000 ¥
N   800 ¥
O   1200 ¥
P   600 ¥
Q   1600 ¥
R   900 ¥

Current practices of *cheng zhong cun* redevelopment also strengthen traditional collective identities, albeit within an urban context. This fact importantly underscores one of the mechanisms through which the simultaneous reconstitution of rural institutions—whether through migrant labor or through actual construction projects—has predicated urbanization in Shenzhen.

This is the case in Baishizhou. The Lvgem Group, a Shenzhen based development company, is proposing to make a new urban entity that aligns itself with a future vision of a modernized, rich, and leisured Shenzhen, finally emancipated from its industrial and informal precursor. The vision consists of razing Baishizhou in its entirety and replacing it with over 5.5 million square meters of real estate.[7] Critically, the people who have made the most money in the loophole of development, the original villagers, are not the inhabitants of the dormitory blocks or the handshakes. Of the 140,000 people who live in Baishizhou, it is estimated that only 2,000 of them are the original villagers. The remaining majority who choose to live in Baishizhou because of its central location, cheap rents, access to the subway, and easy access to employment are the working poor.[8]

Assimilator

Usually migrants, the working poor, are the workers who service the city. They are the street cleaners, security guards, shop assistants, waiters, kitchen hands, massage workers, hotel staff, factory employees, or shopkeepers. For many rural migrants, urban villages like Baishizhou are the first places they go to when they enter the city. They are the transition points between the rural and the urban. They allow for migrants to become assimilated into the city through networks of family and friends that provide contacts for jobs and places to live. Often migrants from the same province end up congregating together, speaking the same dialect, and opening restaurants serving their local cuisine. In this regard urban villages represent sites of adaptation from a rural way of life to the urban that also allows for a connection back to the rural through familiarity and kinship. This reciprocity between the urban and rural pervades the critical role these villages play in China's emergent urban development.

In Shenzhen, the "village" and its "villagers" is a double category. On the one hand, indigenous Shenzhen villages and villagers represent the wealthy future of China's rural population. On the other hand, migrant workers from inland villages to Shenzhen's *cheng zhong cun* are legally still villagers. Moreover, their laboring bodies and absent (but implicitly impoverished homes) represent the conditions that urbanization in Shenzhen aims to transcend, begging the question of how to negotiate the transition from one state of rural being to a future state, when this transformation entails erasing the rural from Shenzhen's landscape. Moreover, the question becomes acutely difficult when we remember that the *cheng zhong cun* are not rural in layout, programs, and population, but rather are rural in memory and by way of the bodies of rural migrants. Thus, the *cheng zhong cun* simultaneously "re-present" both China's rural past and its triumphant transvaluation to diverse audiences—villagers, rural migrants, developers, officials, and migrants from Chinese other major cities.

Developing urban regions undergoing rapid economic growth have always necessitated an influx of migrants from rural areas to the cities. With this comes the inherent problem of how to house this new population. For governments,

7   O'Donnell, Mary Ann. 2013. "Laying Siege to the Villages: Lessons from Shenzhen." *Open Democracy*. 28 March 2013. Accessed March 2013, http://www.opendemocracy.net/opensecurity/mary-ann-o%E2%80%99donnell/laying-siege-to-villages-lessons-from-shenzhen

8   Siu, Helen F. 1989. "Socialist Peddlers and Princes in a Chinese Market Town." *American Ethnologist*. Vol. 16, No. 2, pp. 195–212

← pp. 30/31: Tactics of the working poor in Baishizhou urban village

such a burden on resources for an intangible, fluctuating population is impracticable. In response, settlement areas grow haphazardly to meet the demand, resulting in squatter settlements and slum-like conditions. In contrast, urban villages present an alternative model that mutually benefits the original villagers, the migrants, and the city government. Original villagers profit financially, migrants benefit from the village acting as a staging post and providing relatively cheap rental accommodation, and governments benefit as, in effect, vast amounts of affordable housing is built without them having to pay a single yuan. The model can accommodate fluctuations in the economy and the resultant change in numbers of migrants. As a result, urban villages are not only embedded in the physical morphology of the city but are also entrenched within the urban metabolism of the city itself. If they were eradicated where would the working poor live? How could the city accommodate variations in the influx of migrant workers? And how could rural migrants become assimilated into the operations of the city?

→ Ms. Chi, landlady of Mao era dormitory houses

↘ Interviews were conducted with migrant workers such as this shop owner

Spaces are present within urban villages that do not exist in the more formalized, planned city that surrounds them. The density and proximity to activities within a walkable, almost pedestrianized neighborhood simply do not occur in the homogeneity of Shenzhen's planned city that encapsulates the villages. In some cases, these islands become renowned for offering particular services. The "second-mistress village," (Huang Bei Ling), close to the border crossing at Man Kam To, was a famous center for prostitution as a stopping-off point for truck drivers on their way to, or on their return from, Hong Kong.

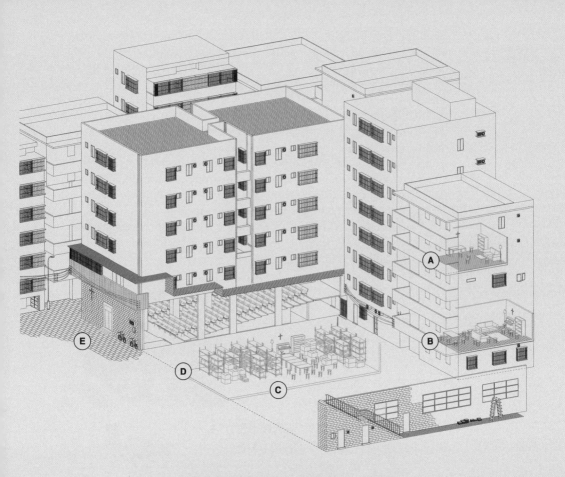

Baishizhou is not infamous in this way but is variegated in the possibilities of urban life: there are night markets; open air pool-tables; factories that have been converted to shopping streets; karaoke bars; food stands; and no doubt prostitutes and gambling dens. There is also a church that occupies the ground and first floor of a typical handshake building. Religion is sensitive in China, with informal gatherings of people of the same religion in non-registered locations deemed illegal. However, many unofficial "house-churches" exist as informal gathering spaces for Christian groups. Depending on current government sentiment, these are either tolerated or cracked down on. The church in Baishizhou became officially registered in 2008; however the congregation evolved from a house-church that began in 1993 in Xintang village. This process describes the potential of the urban village to act as an incubator for alternative programs or activities that wouldn't typically be found in the more rigidly organized and more closely scrutinized formal city. To this extent, they offer a platform for alternative voices, independent groups, or support networks. By implication, they pose a potential, clandestine threat to authority. This unease in control no doubt fuels the government's desire to remove these incredibly troublesome anomalies and replace them with more homogeneously planned, neo-liberal developments.

A   A group of middle-aged women in Xintang village, Baishizhou organized regular gatherings at a believer's home. This marks the beginning of the underground gathering of the church.

B   More members, including a large number of immigrant believers, joined the gathering.

C   As the group grew, Xintang Village Committee offered to support the church through providing an old warehouse as a venue.

D   The old warehouse was converted into a main hall for services. Offices and classrooms are located on the second floor.

E   In 2008, the church was formally approved and licensed by the Ethnic and Religious Affairs Bureau of Shenzhen.

Preservation or Evolution?

Many critics of urban development in Shenzhen have called for another attitude toward urban villages and revel in their manifestation of informal urbanism. Yet aren't these villages themselves examples of untrammeled capitalism with no regard for quality of space, light, air, communal public space, nature, infrastructure, or the living conditions of the inhabitants? The predilection for a seemingly bottom-up process often obfuscates what in reality is an expression of opportunistic profiteering. However, in terms of evaluating the resultant urban form, it is worth considering the recent urban development models that surround Baishizhou.

The surrounding urban fabric around Baishizhou is made up of distinct patches of often gated, privatized developments. Each patch often contains a singular building typology such as the suburban villas of the Portofino development—a luxury residential enclave undertaken by the Overseas Chinese Town development company and modeled on an Italianate villa theme. Increasingly, more physical boundaries are being erected that clearly demarcate these distinct development sites. In some instances these divisions create extreme spatial divides. A 2- to 3-meter-high wall separates Portofino from Baishizhou to maintain the theme-park environment of the residential enclave. Reminiscent of the edge-wall depicted in the movie *The Truman Show*, these walls create visual and spatial boundaries protecting one from any external distractions of the real city outside. The walls also operate to segregate different income groups, social networks, and different citizen status between migrants and non-migrants. The tendency for this mode of gated compound creates homogeneity over differentiation, prioritizing controlled and predictable urban outcomes via single entities such as government supported developers, as opposed to multiple actors or stakeholders. This creates urban neighborhoods that are highly polarized between the rich and the poor, and results in the proliferation of privatized territorial islands amid a discontinuous urban public realm.

↖ The evolution of
Baishizhou church,
Xintang village

↘ Wall separating
Baishizhou Village
from Windows of the
World theme park

In contrast, despite its frenzied capitalistic growth, the urban village has been construed by multiple actors to create a diverse urban landscape, the merits of which have been previously discussed. Are there any strategies that could be used to ensure the future evolution of urban villages rather than their erasure? Or are there urban design tactics that could be implemented in the design of new urban areas?

One strategy would be to maintain the multiple plots and ownerships, within urban villages. This allows multiple stakeholders to engage in the urbanization process, intrinsically creating variation even within a dominant typology such as the handshakes. Buildings within urban villages that face streets often have an overhanging first floor which creates a semi-covered outdoor space at street level. This carved out space is occupied by street vendors, shops, or restaurants, actively promoting economic activities and employment for local inhabitants. This method could be deployed within the design of urban blocks, offering different scaled voids to encourage commercial activity from different actors. Baishizhou also exhibits public spaces that are indeterminate in their programming. In contrast to the heavily monitored, controlled, and fixed occupancy of public spaces in planned developments, these spaces can be used for numerous activities that change according to the time of day or the desires of the inhabitants.

↙ Indeterminate
  public space

↓ Programming
  residual

In terms of policy and regulation, the government clearly finds the status of urban villages to be problematic. However, perhaps their enclave status and differentiation from the rest of the city could be used advantageously as test sites for experimental planning policies. For example, they could be used to try new environmental regulations or promote incentives for people to build with improved access to light and ventilation. In the same way that SEZ's are regarded as experimental urban laboratories within China, could not urban villages be envisaged as micro-sites of experimentation within the city?

Urban villages have been a critical mechanism in China's urbanization process. By providing a space of mediation between the rural and the urban, urban villages were sites for assimilation and adaptation. However, the evolution of the urban village has been halted by policy changes. The palimpsest and historical register of urban change has ceased to evolve. Rather than simply discontinuing their emergence as incubators of urban experimentation, perhaps their different status could offer an alternative urban model than the current mode of increasingly gated and polarized compounds. Without any such spaces of mediation China's urban landscape will be defined by an urban elite and a peripheral working poor. Through localized strategic frameworks that allow for incremental planning rather than metropolitan master plans, there is an opportunity to harness the differentiation, individuality, and entrepreneurial zeal found in urban villages such as Baishizhou.

Yongxin Village

CITY IN THE VILLAGE

In May 2010, we were approached by the Yanai Foundation to develop a prototype for secondary schools in Jiangxi Province. The Yanai Foundation is the charity of a Hong Kong self-made billionaire. At that time he had committed his charity to build one hundred schools in China within just five years. The idea was to develop a design that could adapt to variations in program as well as different site conditions. These schools respond to changing developments in government state sponsored education. Rather than building small individual schools, these schools are part of a new wave of large live-in schools at a county level. They are also prototypes: they comply with the strict codes and regulations for school design throughout China to invent a new school typology.

Change in School Policy

In the past the term "Hope School" has been synonymous with charitable practices in China. Since the implementation of the nine-year compulsory education policy in 1986, there has been a country-wide push to build and receive donations for schools in remote rural areas. One of the first NGOs in China, the China Youth Development Foundation established its flagship program "Project Hope" in 1989 and within the first six years built over 12,000 primary schools. But it has not lasted. Often this wave of building has resulted in the abandonment of schools. This is due in part to the one-child policy resulting in smaller numbers of primary school children as well as overestimation of pupil numbers in order to attract foreign donations. Frequently functional for only a few years, the "Hope Schools" have endemically fallen into disrepair, closed down, or simply been transformed into livestock farms, storage, or government offices. The result is a general disillusionment among donors and increasing pressure on the government to regulate these projects.

Partially motivated by the May 12 earthquake in Sichuan Province, which exposed the corruption and poor construction of hundreds of "Hope Schools," the central government is currently endorsing a policy of school consolidation. This is happening on two levels. One combines small primary schools to form larger primary school clusters. Another groups students together into newly built mega schools composed of 2,000–4,000 students, including live-in dormitories housing primary and secondary school children. These schools are located closer to cities and reflect an attempt at greater top-down control and regulation of school administration and pedagogy. It is a shift in focus from the rural to the urban and as the example of our second prototype shows, the schools are often part of an ambitious planning proposal for entirely new-built towns. The school therefore plays an integral part in the process of rural urbanization.

Two Very Different Sites

Both of our prototype schools are located in Yongxin County. One school is located in the midst of a small village while another is in the midst of a newly built town center. Both schools draw students from throughout the county. A single design would have to work in two extreme sites, one rural and one urban. The concept for the design is to treat the school itself as a village community.

↙ Construction of foundations for the school in Sanmeng Village

↓ Sanmeng Village school site

↑ View of Suichang Town

At least 2,000 students would live and work in the school. Even students who live over 500 meters away will be required to live on campus from Monday through Friday. Students living farther away will stay the entire semester. This creates a community of students that by population is greater than their home villages. The design tries to create a programmatic and spatial sense of community.

In China, the political division of land occurs in five primary layers beginning with the province, followed by the city, county, town, and village. Yongxin County has planned a total of five large primary and secondary schools. Within the county there are thirty-six townships, and within each town, up to ten villages. The first of the schools is located in the village of Sanmeng. With a total of 3,000 students and 2,000 of them living on campus, the school population effectively doubles the size of Sanmeng Village, which is composed of around 1,000 families. The question was how to deal with this collision of scale.

The second prototype school is in the township of Suichang, located in the center of an entirely newly planned area. The school site at the time of construction was already surrounded by the skeleton structures of high-rise residential towers. Billboards with big renderings placed at future street intersections were the only markers helping to visualize the ambitious future urban area. During the time of the first site visit, a 4-meter-high blanket of earth was being systematically applied over the rice fields. This would become the foundation for the new town, containing drainage and other infrastructural pipes. By creating an entirely new datum covering the rice fields, it would also wipe away all that existed from before.

Walled City

Beginning with these two opposing sites our main design question was how to make a single school design, essentially a city built within a village and a village within the city center. Our initial reaction was to create a perimeter building that encloses a large plaza. This wall, much like a traditional old city wall, frames the inner public life of the school and creates a strong distinction with the outside. This simple idea however violated existing school building regulations. In China, all school buildings regardless of their location must have a north-south orientation. This results in schools with strict rows of buildings that often do not relate to their surrounding environment. After many discussions, we finally resolved the issue by orienting all rooms (dorms and classrooms) at a 45-degree angle to the building facade. This way we could still preserve a square plan arrangement, and have all rooms facing the same north-south direction. Corridors would run along the inside of the perimeter. The result is that from certain angles, the entire outer wall would seem impenetrable with no windows showing. It lacked a sense of scale. We decided to tile this facade in a design that alludes to the mountains behind. Instead of breaking down the scale of the program into individual buildings, the wall created an abstract backdrop—its own individual context—that allowed each project to have an interesting resonance in either the city or the countryside.

Social Landscape

If our first action in the design was to build up the school as a single enclosure, then the second was to break down the interior courtyard into a series of smaller-scaled spaces. Additional public and social functions of the school such as the library, the canteen, the art block, and the administration building, protrude into this space activating the courtyard. The courtyard space acts

↓ Courtyard of
Sanmeng school

as a *campus*—an interconnected space for living, working, and socializing. The campus is further divided into smaller spaces that relate to each of the social functions to create micro-communities within the larger space. For the prototype we proposed a variety of different types of buildings that can be used interchangeably. Each building is essentially a landscape building, designed with a specific sectional concept that relates it to the ground. These buildings contribute a great deal to the social life of students. They don't merely house programs, they are public buildings. The library rises up from the ground as a series of steps leading to an outdoor terrace, the canteen is cantilevered forming a pleasant shaded area for dining, the art block has an inner courtyard allowing the classroom activities to spill outside during good weather, and the office block has a multi-function meeting room that receives light from both sides.

For this project, we had to change our approach to school design. As a reaction against generic school buildings, we always approached each project with the intention to create a very site-specific design. However, the prescribed requirements in this project were different. Not only is the scale in another order of magnitude (nearly ten times the size of typical primary school projects) the demand is for a prototype that allows itself to be duplicated. Balancing these requirements, the challenge for the design is to be flexible without becoming generic. We hoped to achieve this by designing for a range of social building types that could be implemented in the large central plaza in order to define different landscape conditions. The large "city wall" frames

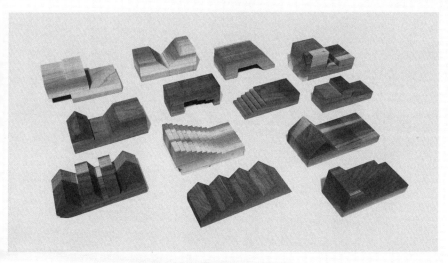

↗ Models of various school building prototypes

→ The design exploration begins with a series of interlocking buildings.

these unique landscapes on the inside but presents a visually responsive backdrop to the exterior condition—whether it is urban or rural.

← pp. 42/43: Exterior view of Sanmeng school

After these two initial prototypes, the contract with the donor was not continued. In fact, he simply hired our project architect to carry out the remaining designs. Discontinuation was also in the interest of the Local Design Institute, who worked with an extremely low fee to prepare the construction documents for our design. Often it is the case that our concern with detail and quality creates (from their point of view) unnecessary work. The government was interested in the speed of construction. The donor was invested in the goal of one hundred school buildings. The fact that our desire to make quality, site-specific architecture encountered difficulty is not surprising. In a Chinese context, the struggle to balance huge development goals while striving to cater more individually to specific social, economic, and environmental conditions is the current challenge for rural development.

← The ground floor functions as a covered recreational space, filled with Ping Pong tables and other activities.

↙ The ground floor of the school block is open, with a view of the landscape.

Factory Village

A NEW INDUSTRIAL PARADIGM

In the 1990s the Pearl River Delta (PRD) became known as the World's Factory. It produced vast quantities of shoes, garments, plastic toys, furniture, household goods, domestic appliances, computer bits, buttons, gaskets, and unnameable component parts that facilitate our modern, consumer-convenient lives. This widespread urbanization linked to industrialization created urban centers with populations greater than some of the largest cities in the Western world (both Guangzhou and Shenzhen have populations well over 10 million inhabitants). Fuelled by the relatively buoyant global economy and the West's continued desire for mass-produced goods, this period of unparalleled growth was faced in the early 2000s with a period of economic fragility due to a global recession that even China could not bypass. This article investigates how this downturn affected factory sites in the PRD and contrasts its susceptibility to collapse when compared to two historic, industrial cities; Manchester and Detroit. In both those cities, the processes of urbanization were different and attributable to separate paradigmatic shifts in the evolution of industrialization: from the industrial revolution to the mass assembly line. As new paradigms emerge, new forces transform the existing city, restructuring and reconfiguring its previous organization leading to shifts in economic geography, political control, migration, infrastructure, and built fabric.

This essay will question whether the current urbanization processes occurring in the PRD are simply a continuation along the axis of late 20th-century industrialization or represent a paradigmatic shift. If so, is it a predicatable model; is it an amalgam of previous processes; what are its characteristics; or is something altogether new happening? Can the urbanization processes in the PRD be considered part of this lineage and emblematic of the global, industrial city of the 21st century?

Globalized Industrialization in the PRD

The Third Plenum of the Eleventh Central Committee of the Chinese Communist Party (CCP) meetings of 1978 initiated a new era of reform in China with Deng Xiao Peng as its key instigator. Structured around Four Modernizations—

agriculture, industry, national defense, and science and technology—
the reforms brought about a loosening of state control and an engagement
with foreign entities at a government and commercial level. These reforms
represented China's gradual "opening up" and as such allowed the processes
of globalization to play a critical role in China's development. Originally, the
reforms were centered on initiating rural changes—restructuring the collective
farm system creating incentives for farmers to both branch into other sectors
and also allowing them to sell any surplus produce over the required state
quotas at market prices. This shift from the collective to the individual was
also reflected in industry, allowing factory managers to have more control over
their workforce, output, and potential side-line industries and to also produce
beyond state-quotas. Rhetorically, "capitalist" forces were used to trigger
"socialist production." [1]

    This stirring of market forces at the level of rural peasants was
matched by a new era of foreign policy. Engagement with the United States
signaled a new opening of trade relations. At the same time that the United
States completely severed formal diplomatic ties with Taiwan, China ordered
planes from Boeing and signed a deal with Coca-Cola allowing the sale
of their product in China. Taiwan itself was pragmatically seen as a model
for economic growth; in 1979 it had only 8% of the PRC's total population,
six times its GNP. [2] The Taiwanese had created Export Processing Zones
that created favorable conditions for trade exports, stimulating an influx
of foreign investment. This model was appropriated and re-branded by Deng
Xiao Peng as Special Economic Zones (SEZ) and in 1979 four were launched.

1 Spence, Jonathan D.
1999. *The Search for
Modern China*, W. W.
Norton & Company,
New York, London

2 ibid. p. 632

↙ Typical factory site in
the Pearl River Delta

3   Sassen, Saskia. 1991.
    "The Global City." In
    *The Global City: New
    York, London, Tokyo,*
    Princeton University
    Press, New Jersey

4   Statistics Bureau of
    Guangdong Province.
    "2010 6th National
    Census, Guangdong
    Province Data Report."
    28 April 2011. Accessed
    12 June 2013. http://
    www.stats.gov.cn/tjgb/
    rkpcgb/qgrkpcgb/t201
    10428_402722232.htm

Shenzhen was one of these. Although a predominantly agricultural county, Shenzhen was strategically located directly across the border from Hong Kong, by then an established global financial center.

Through these shifts in policy, Deng foresaw the potential for China to act as fertile territory for the expression of late capitalism in built form: the continued commodification of goods, worldwide consumption and expanded field of production centers made possible through globalization, prioritized affordable and available land, cooperative governmental controls, and an abundance of cheap labor. Saskia Sassen argues in *The Global City*[3] that the 1960s marked a period of restructuring the world's economy that led to the collapse of traditional industrial strongholds in the United Kingdom and the United States, the rapid industrialization of the third world, and the transformation of the financial industry into an international transactional network that repositioned certain cities as new centers within this global system. These nodes centralized activities acting as control points providing specialized services such as law, financial services, management, and technological innovation. Hong Kong acted as a key node and facilitator for companies to embark upon decentralized production within the PRD that took advantage of the cheap land, cheap labor, and tax breaks offered by the SEZ.

This abundance of available labor was fuelled by a growing migrant population that began to flock to the new centers of production of the SEZ's, which was encouraged by a later policy in 1983 that allowed rural citizens to work in designated urban areas legally without changing their citizen status. Additional policy changes were brought about by Document Number 1 in 1984 that further evolved market forces. Again these were embedded in rural organizations allowing collective investment into joint enterprises and for villagers to have control over land use and development rights. These initiatives were instrumental in promoting urbanization through rural agents. The interconnectivity between local rural collectives, the economic desirability of the SEZ's, and the forces of the global market created the conditions for unprecedented urbanization. Shenzhen SEZ acted as a mediator between global entities and local enterprises with rural collectives or individuals acting as opportunistic and entrepreneurial agents for industrial production, land use contracting, or property development. In 1984 the PRD was formalized as one of three development triangles alongside the Min River Delta (Fujian) and the Yangtze River Delta (Shanghai), targeted for continued economic growth. This stimulated competition between cities to gain foreign investment with newer, second tier towns, such as Dongguan, directly undercutting costs of Shenzhen, allowing the city to develop extremely fast. Spurred on by the globalization of markets, the rapid urbanization of these production centers within the PRD created an industrial amalgam that became known as the World's Factory. This initiated vast flows of migrant workers to the region, which was estimated in 2010 to be in excess of 30 million in Guangdong Province alone.[4]

Such unbridled urbanization related to industrialization has not been witnessed in equal intensity since the advent of the world's first industrialized city: 19th-century Manchester. If Manchester exhibited a specific form of urbanization related to industrial processes in the 19th century, we can see an equally unique form of urban growth occurring in the 20th century in the example of Detroit: The Motor City. Both Manchester and Detroit emerged

from particular industrial contexts that shaped their urban form. In each case globalization became an increasingly important emergent force that acted to transform each city through periods of boom or bust. By summarizing the historical evolution of industrialization in Manchester and Detroit the objective is to position the processes occurring in the PRD in this contextual frame.

↖ Urban periphery, Dongguan, 2009

The Industrial City in Context

Manchester between 1750 and 1900 was a city that emerged as a by-product of untrammelled capitalism arising from the industrial production of cotton. It was the first time the processes of the city and urbanization became directly linked to the processes of industrialization. Operating like a borderless SEZ, Manchester and its region had loose governmental controls, an open economy for investment and entrepreneurship, a constellation of existing trades from weavers to engineering companies, as well as an influx of cheap labor from Ireland. The period of invention in technology furthered production methods, setting up new social relations between worker and industrialist through the mechanism of the factory. As a result the population trebled between 1774 and 1801.[5] The graphic portrayal of the city of Manchester in 1853 by Engels[6] described a city organized according to the inequality produced by these new social relations: the slum dwellings of migrant workers located behind the facade of merchant warehouses protected the new bourgeoisie from having to witness the conditions endemic to the new system.

    The key characteristics of this industrial revolution—the coupling of cheap labor alongside mechanical invention—together with increased global influences, ultimately engendered Manchester's inevitable downfall. The end of the First World War opened up new markets and released control of textile production in British colonies, such as India, bringing competition to Manchester's textile trade and a fluctuating, volatile market. The increased

5 Hall, Peter. 1998. "The First Industrial City: Manchester 1760–1830." In *Cities in Civilisation*, Pantheon Books, New York

6 Engels, Friedrich. 1845. "The Great Towns." In *The Condition of the Working Class in England*, translated and edited by W. O. Henderson and W. H. Chaloner, Basil Blackwell, 1958

possibility of global competition, as well as technological advances in the United States, set about a slow burn of economic decline that was to continue throughout the 20th century. The further decentralization of factories and suburbanization post World War II, coupled with large scale urban planning strategies promoting satellite towns and tabula housing developments, attempted to reconfigure Manchester's industrial legacy. However the continued demise of the city (right up until the late 1980s) was predicated on the city's inability to compete with new global industrial processes or to evolve its industrial base.

If Manchester fell victim to the first phase of globalization, then Detroit was a casualty of phase two. Detroit's rapid urban growth was in direct correlation to the boom of the motor-car industry in line with new mechanisms of productivity brought about by Ford's mass assembly line. The influx of migrant laborers from America's South as well as from Canada, England, and Poland meant that in 1900, one in three Detroiters was an immigrant. Further waves of migration occurred because of the economic

↑ Foxconn, Longhuazhen, 2010

↗ Manchester's industrial legacy, 2010

attraction of Ford's five dollar basic wage and five-day working week. In 1917 Ford's River Rouge Plant was the world's largest factory employing 100,000 workers. This can be compared today with Foxconn—a manufacturer of hi-tech microchips and components, located in Longhuazhen, Shenzhen—which has a factory population of over 400,000 (approximately equivalent to the current population of Manchester's central district). Unlike in Manchester, the workers now had money to spend, creating an economic cycle of productivity and consumption that defined the machinations of market capitalism. Indeed Ford's dream was "to build a car for the great multitude."

Post-war decentralization was exacerbated by the Federal Highway Act of 1956 extending the highway infrastructure allowing simultaneous suburbanization and relocation of factories. This, coupled with racial tension and housing policies that favored homogeneity, meant that the city was gradually abandoned, suffering a 50% loss of population from 1950 to 1990 with the city center transformed from being 85% white to 85% black. The failure of the city to expand and annex the wealthier suburbs meant that the city lost huge taxable revenues both from businesses and from the population. This created a vicious cycle whereby the lack of civic funds exacerbated the inability of the city to attract investment or improve public services, perpetuating the exodus to the suburbs. Industrial processes also evolved characterizing the second phase of globalization into a more networked and sub-contracted model. Not only were factories located in suburban areas but also parts could be manufactured wherever there was cheaper labor, abundant and economical land, or easier access to raw materials and specializations. There were few advantages to being in the city and Detroit lost out in the global competitive market to act as a hub for this distributed mode of production. In addition the susceptibility to global economic changes, such as the oil crisis of the 1970, as well as increased global competition from Japanese carmakers decimated Detroit's manufacturers and furthered the city's decline. Despite efforts to re-invent the city and attract investment, the city continued to lose an estimated 250,000 people between 2000 and 2010 and was declared to be bankrupt in 2013.[7]

The examples of Manchester and Detroit illustrate both the development of urban growth related to distinct sectors of industrialization (textiles and the motorcar) and the effect of globalization in terms of production and in terms of the adverse susceptibility of the marketplace. Both cities exhibited extreme forms of urban shrinkage that left their city cores abandoned, with a legacy of vacated industrial factories, warehouses, and plants.

7   Williams, Corey. "Detroit is broke; could bankruptcy lie ahead?" *The Guardian*. 13 May 2013. Accessed May 2013. http:// www.guardian.co.uk/ commentisfree/2013/ jul/21/how-detroit-was-laid-low?INTCMP =SRCH

Network Model of Production

In this context the PRD region can be considered as an example of a third phase of urbanization related to industrialization that has been defined by, and constructed from, processes of globalization. Notably different from the previous historical examples, the current model is based on a constellation of urban hubs within a regional network of industrial production, rather than on individual cities.

↖ Downtown Detroit, 2002

8   Castells, Manuel. 1989. "The Informational Mode of Development and the Restructuring of Capitalism." In *The Informational City: information Technology, Economic Restructuring, and the Urban-Regional Process*, Blackwell, Oxford

Castells in his 1989 book *The Informational City* [8] argues that the new condition of the global economy is constructed from the emergence of an increasingly networked society through what he describes as the "informational mode of development" and a requisite restructuring of capitalism. He makes the argument that the technological advances and creation of a new information infrastructure of computers and telecommunications allows for production to be less dependent on the specificity of a location. It also facilitates ease of relocation and increased flexibility for expansion or cxontraction. Skilled labor, natural resources, and localized knowledge are no longer the defining factors in situating the centers of industrial production. The predominant factors are the availability of extensive land areas, a large and easily replenished labor force, and favorable and competitive economic policies. Unlike the traditional, highly evolved workers' unions in the examples of Manchester and Detroit, workers within new centers of production, particularly in developing regions and at the initial stage of growth, have little sense of collective workers' rights. New migrants entering these factories directly from the countryside find it hard to know whether they are receiving fair pay, are not being overworked, and are being accommodated in acceptable living conditions when they have nothing to compare it with. However this period is short-lived because of the social connectivity between workers, particularly as many arrive from the same home villages and standards are disseminated through their constant movement searching for better pay, work, and housing facilities (Leslie Chang documents

9   Chang, Leslie T. 2008. *Factory Girls: From Village to City in a Changing China*, Spiegal & Grau, U.S.A.

this quest through the everyday experiences of factory girls in Dongguan). [9] Castells also points out that the networked model of production is likely to be more elastic in nature and more able to negotiate the volatility of the market. When compared to the extreme ramifications of the boom-and-bust cycles on the cotton industry in Manchester and the auto industry in Detroit this seems conceivable, however, at the beginning of 2009, the impact of the global recession was permeating uneasily through the region.

Recession

↗ Signs of potential instability, Dongguan, 2009

This unease was well justified as the scale of such large losses of population due to unemployment were completely unprecedented and their impact unknown. The mode of production in the region was export driven and reliant on the continued demand for consumer goods from the West. As this demand stultified at the end of 2008, many workers were released and factories closed down. As a result the *International Herald Tribune* reported on 6 February 2009 that "20 million of the nation's 130 million migrant workers are unemployed." [10] The media exposed the insecurity of the recession and were quick to link the issue of migrant unemployment with the potential for increased social unrest. For example, the article "Laid-off migrants doomed to suffer in crisis" suggests that the returning workers would "threaten social stability." [11] In investigating one factory complex in Dongguan that exemplifies this model of export-dominated industrial production we visited the site in 2009 at the height of the recession and again in 2013 to first register the impact of the downturn on this complex and, second, to observe whether, five years on, it had renewed its vigor and was back to levels of production and worker numbers that had existed prior to the economic slowdown.

Yuyuan High Tech Opto-electronics Estate was founded in 1993 by Taiwan Baocheng Group—the largest shoe manufacturing enterprise in the world—as a controlled factory complex with eighteen factories in Huangjiang Town, Dongguan. Economic regions such as the PRD and the Yangtze River Delta were pitted against each other to compete to lure enterprises, such as Baocheng, to set up in their areas. Huangjiang was selected owing to the proved success of a local drinks manufacturer, Taiyangshen, as well as cheap land that

10 Bradsher, Keith. "China's Unemployment Swells as Exports Falter." *International Herald Tribune.* 6 February 2009

11 Tam, Fiona. "Laid-off Migrants Doomed to Suffer in Crisis," *South China Morning Post.* 6 January 2009

↑ Yuyuan factory town, 2013

was rented from local village collectives, labor costs of 300 yuan per month and the preferential tax breaks created by the Economic Development Zone set up in Dongguan in 1985. Originally, the first phase was dominated by ten shoe factories of leading global brands, such as Nike and Adidas, however by 1997, Baocheng had diversified and expanded to include electronics and computer components. The location of the factory intersects the collective land from four surrounding villages (Helu, Yuanwuwei, Jitigang, Bei'an) and each villager has been receiving approximately 400 yuan per person per month since 1993.

A gated factory complex, Yuyuan is organized to be self-reliant and autonomous from the surrounding villages, complete with a health center, sports fields, and shops and restaurants. During its peak there were as many as 100,000 workers. In 2009 the number was estimated at 40,000 as a result of the downturn resulting in the closing of commercial facilities and the vacancy

→ Ms. Yin, 2009

↘ Factory canteen, 2013

↓ Factory dormitory, 2013

12 Interview with a local resident Mrs. Chen, 20 March 2009

13 Interview with a local worker Ms. Yin, 20 March 2009

14 "Interpretation on Yucheng Strike." 163 Forum. 18th Nov 2011. Accessed June 2013. http://bbs.news.163 .com/bbs/society/ 237148435.html

15 BBC News. "World Bank Cuts China Growth Forecast." 13 June 2013. Accessed June 2013. http:// www.bbc.co.uk/news/ business-22883830

of factory worker's quarters.[12] Ms. Chen, originally from Gansu province, opened a Sichuan-style restaurant in the commercial street within the Yuyuan compound in 2007. Since the beginning of 2009, job losses have impacted her business and others, with ten shops and restaurants closing down in the same street. In order to attract tenants, Yuyuan cut rents from 5,400 RMB per month to 3,000 RMB per month. A young worker, Ms. Yin,[13] said that despite job losses recruitment is still continuing, however this seems premised on the replacement of dissatisfied workers rather than on expansion. There are about 10,000 workers in her shoe factory working over nine hours a day, five and a half days a week for a wage of 1,100 to 1,300 RMB per month. The current pressure of the marketplace is forcing factory owners to demand more of their workers for less. In October 2011 the Yucheng Shoe Factory made eighteen managers redundant without compensation and overtime hours were cut that led to salary drops of 1,000–2,000 yuan per month. On 18 November, 7,000 factory workers (from an estimated total of 9,000) went on strike. Skirmishes took place between riot police and protesters but by the evening the workers had returned to the factory.[14]

By 2013, the hype and paranoia that escalated in the early months of 2009 about the adverse affect the recession would have on the factories in the PRD had largely dissipated. However, the anticipated renewed vigor of the export market simply has not occurred, the global downturn is still present, and in June 2013 the World Bank cut China's growth forecast based on the decline in demand for export goods from Europe and the United States.[15] For industrial sites, such as Yuyuan, who are heavily dependent on the continued

← Mr. Fang, Haofang
grocery, Yuyuan, 2013

demand for these goods, the impact of the recession has been correspondingly
more protracted and gradual. Visiting the site again in June 2013 we interviewed
several people including Mr. Fang, owner of the Haofang Grocery on Yuyuan
Commercial Street:

> Business on the commercial street used to be great. In the past, Yuyuan had more
> than thirty shops on the street and it was hard for new businesses to get a spot. But
> things have got worse since the financial crisis in 2008: two thirds of the shops have
> moved out and two are closing this month ... Without buyers' orders, the Taiwanese
> factories in Yuyuan are unable to produce and unable to pay ample salary. This
> in turn has affected the buying power of the workers who supported the commercial
> street ... The Sichuan restaurant you visited closed around the summer of 2012 ...

> Mr. Fang attributes these changes to the closure of factories: "Out of the thirty
> something factories in Yuyuan back in the 2000's, there are about fifteen to
> twenty factories left in 2013. Dozens of smaller factories have closed down since
> 2008 ... There used to be around 100,000 workers in Yuyuan, now there are only
> 20,000 working and living here. Specifically, the number of workers in one of the
> factories, Yucheng Shoe-making, has dropped from 18000 to 2300 since 2009.[16]

16 Interview with Mr. Fang,
Yuyuan Commercial
Street, 30 May 2013,
conducted by Wang
Tian Meng

As a shop owner since 2006, Mr. Fang is perceptive about the changing
inhabitants of the factory complex, noticing that the age of the workers has
shifted from teenagers to people in their mid-thirties, who often arrive looking
for work as couples. He also observed a trend for people preferring to live in
accommodation outside the factory, instead choosing to live in nearby villages,
where they are not restricted or governed by regulations preventing workers
from cooking, living as a couple, or enforcing a night-time curfew. He also
reflects that one of the reasons people have stopped coming in such numbers
is due to the urbanization of their inner hometowns: "My village hometown
in Hubei has almost become a small town with roads, industry, and tourism.
It might get even bigger than Huangjiang."

The exception to the closures of commercial shops and restaurants
in Yuyuan was the increased number of vocational training schools. These
schools are private companies that often have strategic partnerships with
factories requiring higher level skilled labor with language and IT training.
In addition these schools are attractive to workers who want to advance into
higher income sector jobs. Staff at the Xinhaobo Vocational Training School
stated: "Modern youth from the countryside are no longer satisfied with

17 Interview with staff at Xinhaobo Vocational Training School, 30 May 2013, conducted by Wang Tian Meng

having a simple job at a factory, working for other people. They would like to open up their own small business, like an online store on Taobao.com or other forms of online marketing, which also requires them to have more professional knowledge than their average high school education." [17]

In many ways the slowdown in Yuyuan is not just a result of the recession, but is also due to the evolution of the industrial sector across China. As early as 2000 the government began promoting the distribution of industrial production to "Open up the West" into China's interior, investing heavily in major infrastructure and energy projects. The PRD is in an increasingly competitive market: the once high wages offered compared to local work can now be achieved for some migrants without having to travel so far from home. Workers themselves are also more selective about where they work and how they can further their career prospects. One couple looking for work in Yuyuan summarized it: "If we can't negotiate to 2,500 yuan per month, we will probably leave town for other places."

In order to compensate for its overreliance on the export market, the PRC government has been trying to encourage domestic consumption. In fact, domestic spending compared to GDP has declined by 10% to just 33% of GDP from 1997 to 2007 and compares to figures of 53% for India and 58% for Brazil.[18] In data from the World Bank from 2011, the figures have not significantly altered: 34% for China, 59% for India, and 60% for Brazil.[19] New policies to encourage spending are being tested that include government discounts on goods such as TV's and domestic appliances, as well as a consideration to overhaul the land rights policy, which could allow rural dwellers use their land as equity, thereby freeing up capital for investment or consumption.

18 Huang, Yasheng. "Reviving China's Rural Miracle." *The Guardian Weekly*. 22 May 2009, p. 19

19 The World Bank. "Household Final Consumption Expenditure, etc. (% of GDP)." Accessed July 2013. http://data .worldbank.org/ indicator/NE.CON .PETC

Transition

These characteristics of third phase industrialization linked to globalization are very different from the preceding examples of Detroit and Manchester. Yuyuan, as a sample site, demonstrates that the model of industrial production that defined the PRD as the World's Factory is now in transition and undergoing a process of evolution. The dual effects of the recession and the government drive to proliferate industry away from the eastern seaboard have meant that many towns are adapting and repositioning themselves as service sector providers, hi-tech parks, green industries, or even tourist destinations.

The extreme urban shrinkage and abandonment of the city-centers of Detroit and Manchester resulted in a crisis of the core in relation to the periphery. Both of these cities were profoundly affected by the dual processes of suburbanization and decentralization of industries, which, among other economic factors, led to urban malaise. In the case of the urban territory in cities such as Dongguan, urban processes are rooted in an already sprawl-like condition—there cannot be a crisis of the core when the city itself has no definable center. Interestingly, unlike these historical cities that evolved through the origination of a city core, areas such as Dongguan only start considering the centralization of the urban core after the peripheral, yet economically productive, sprawl has been established. In Dongguan this recentralization process has led to the iconic construction of a vast civic plaza, an iconic theater designed by a foreign architect, and new government

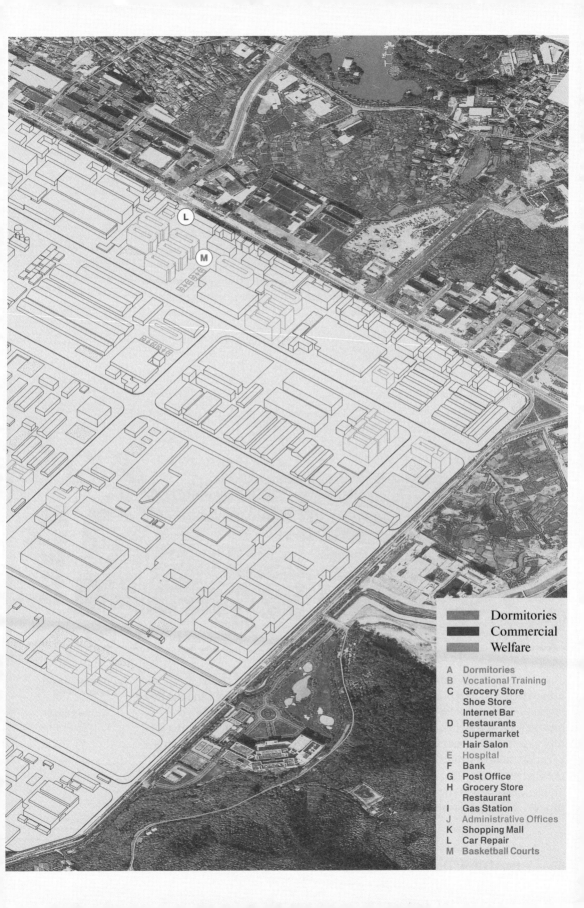

Dormitories
Commercial
Welfare

A   Dormitories
B   Vocational Training
C   Grocery Store
     Shoe Store
     Internet Bar
D   Restaurants
     Supermarket
     Hair Salon
E   Hospital
F   Bank
G   Post Office
H   Grocery Store
     Restaurant
I   Gas Station
J   Administrative Offices
K   Shopping Mall
L   Car Repair
M   Basketball Courts

headquarters: all symbols of centrality that fit a generic idea for a civic locus yet lack the textured richness of variegated urban fabric.

← pp. 56/57: Yuyuan factory complex describing different public programs

If we return to Yuyuan and the town of Huangjiang within Dongguan, the formal urban planning has had four stages. The first up until 2000 is recognized by the planners as in-situ urbanization—a free-for-all and establishment of industrially productive land from farmland. The second stage and first master plan in 2001 was developed to improve infrastructure through the creation of a main north-south axis with the objective of switching to specializing in electronics' production. In 2004 this master plan was revised to create two additional cross streets splitting the area into three identifiable zones. The third master plan for 2010–20 concentrated on the town center, developing light-rail, preserving the natural landscape, and shifting from a manufacturing to a service base, with the intent to "lift the town-center beyond a mere administrative and commercial platform." Lifestyle, ecology, and tourism are the new buzzwords. However, such a vision seems inconceivable while travelling on nondescript highways, past intrusive electric pylons needed to serve the power requirements of factories, and alongside decimated hillsides and vast tracts of sullied landscapes.

↑ Dongguan town center, 2009

↗ Workers taking a break, 2009

So, can we consider this model of 21st century industrialized urbanization to be a paradigm shift? The industrialized processes themselves fall within the model of decentralized, global capital made possible by information-led technologies as described by Castells. The effect of globalized processes seeking out ever cheaper land and labor also ties in with the pattern of industrial expansion expressed through the outward movement within the PRD from Shenzhen to Dongguan and later at a national scale from the eastern seaboard to the western provinces. However it is the urbanization process itself, that is most different from the precedents of either Manchester or Detroit, particularly with respect to the coupling of top-down policy (for example, the formation of the SEZ) and bottom-up development. In addition the mechanisms of adapting to the economic downturn have had a very different effect. The recession in the PRD has been profound, as the example of Huangjiang testifies, with many losing their jobs and returning home to the countryside. However this impact has been moderated by the capability of rural areas to act as sponges, absorbing vast numbers of migrants when necessary and returning them when the economic outlook changes. Simultaneously the recession in the PRD correlated with a top-down intention to re-colonize and urbanize these areas, transforming them from industrial hinterlands into examples of Chinese modernity with well-connected infrastructure, non-polluting factories, and a leisured, ecologically minded populace. This has been exemplified by China's massive economic stimulus package, under way since 2008, that has included an investment (announced in 2012) in infrastructure alone worth 157 billion U.S. dollars.[20] This ability to pour vast amounts of financial capital into restructuring this urbanized territory was simply not possible in the economic aftermath that plagued the shrinking conditions of Manchester and Detroit. These cities were left to fend

20 Sweney, Pete, and Langi Chiang. "China Approves $157-billion Infrastructure Spending." Reuters. September 12 2012. Accessed July 2013. http://www.reuters.com/ article/2012/09/07/ us-chinaeconomydUSB RE88613C20120907

for themselves in open competition with other cities countrywide or from around the world. For these cities their industrial demise has been prolonged and gradual: for Manchester, one could argue it exceeded one hundred years; for Detroit, over fifty. Despite Manchester's regeneration and successful reinvention the impact of post-industrial collapse still underpins the urban fabric of the city. In Detroit its infamy as a ruin is still its dominant identity. For the towns and cities within the urban amalgam across the PRD the next phase of development is still open-ended. However it is remarkable that such unknown and relatively small towns as Huangjiang have such grand plans for their reinvention. Whether these visions will remain as hyperbole, founded on an unrealistic image of the future given the reality of the industrially scarred earth, remains to be seen.

Based on this reading of the PRD in relation to the historical precedents of Manchester and Detroit, the emergence of a new paradigm for industrial urbanization is evidenced in two ways. First the simultaneous application of large-scale policy with bottom-up village-led industrial development is unique. Second, the government's intention to recentralize and form city-centers as a last step in the urbanization process represents a very different model from the other examples. However, the present policy of implementing top-down plans without harnessing the potential of pro-active individuals or village entities is a missed opportunity. This represents a reversion to established urban planning models that undermines the potential of this paradigm to evolve in a distinct and productive way.

↖ Factory town, 2009

Lingzidi Village

RESOLVING INFRASTRUCTURAL CONFLICTS

↗ A rest-stop along the highway, including a gas station, hotel and entertainment facilities

Throughout China the government is investing huge amounts of capital in the construction of infrastructure. The high speed rail and highway networks are extending to remote towns and villages making the economic urban centers more and more accessible. In their wake, mountains are flattened, earth is extracted, tunnels dug, and a vast array of flyovers, viaducts, and intersections are implanted across the countryside. Not only is this bringing rural migrants into cities, this is bringing the urbanization process directly into villages.

Highway Urbanism

This process is largely welcomed by villagers as it creates new employment opportunities. The mass migration of workers to and from cities has resulted in a landscape of movement, creating a type of highway urbanism. As arterial roads are constructed through village land, many villages opt to move their houses or build commercial shop houses along these roads. These roads have essentially become the production lines of the city. Materials for construction originate in the village, may be further refined in other village factories along the way, and are finally sold in roadside warehouses. Villages are abandoning their agricultural production in favor of specializing in material production, processing, and even shipping. Often an entire village along with every villager will specialize in the production of a single building material. In one particular village located an hour's drive north of Guangzhou, every house has a blue truck parked in front of it. It has become a village of lorry drivers.

↑ Drying wood veneer in front of a factory

↖ A village of lorry drivers with trucks parked in front of each house

Recently, vast elevated infrastructural systems built primarily to link urban populations are causing disruptions within the rural landscape. These networks can paradoxically cause spatial, social, and economic barriers. Though built high above the ground to avoid confrontation with local conditions, there are inevitably problems. An example is a project site in southern Shaanxi Province where the construction of a new highway literally cut through the center of a river valley resulting in the destruction of hundreds of existing local bridges. Our project brief involved the design of new pedestrian bridges to reconnect the local population living on either side of this river valley. These new bridges have to negotiate not only the steep slope of the valley but also the space beneath the highway and above a river. In the past where a simple rope bridge was sufficient, the solution now required complex spatial maneuvers.

↘ A project site for
a pedestrian bridge
situated directly
underneath the highway

↓ New highway
construction along
a river valley

Program Bridges

Our approach to these spatially difficult sites was to create a series of bridges that would intensify the idea of infrastructural connection through providing additional programs. For each village we designed a site-specific combination of pedestrian and vehicular traffic routes. These designs expand the program of the bridge: one design extends up a slope and provides a viewing deck, while another wraps underneath itself to give access to the riverbed for clothes' washing, and a third crosses over itself so the stepped passage can be used as a seating area. Instead of a neutral concrete slab, each bridge provides an additional social function and creates one small-scale public space in the village. Against the scale of an increasingly mega-infrastructure, our reaction is to propose interventions at a micro-scale.

↙ Bridge designs for three different site conditions

↓ Model of Lingzidi bridge

↑ Construction of the Lingzidi bridge underneath an elevated highway

↗ Discussion with villagers about the bridge design

Recently constructed in 2013, the bridge design for Lingzidi Village is situated directly underneath a new railway connection between Xian to Nanjing. It is part of a larger infrastructure strategy linking Xian to Shangzhou and Shangzhou to the villages. Despite this new large-scale development, the actual infrastructure within the villages remains inadequate with no provision for sewage or running water. The villagers received around 1,600 RMB (200 USD) per family for the loss of their agricultural land, though many complained that this was insufficient. The removal of a portion of the mountain for construction of the rail-line has led to an increase in flood water into the river valley during rainy seasons. In 2010, the flood destroyed a small bridge that used to connect farmland to the village. Despite its small scale this bridge was a critical node in the trade network that allowed produce to be transported from the fields to nearby markets.

Our task was to redesign this bridge to reconnect the nearby walnut orchard to the road infrastructure and thereby preserve the village economy. The concept of the bridge was a singular loop that would link two levels of the riverbanks with an additional connection to the river. In effect this produces a wide, direct path for small trucks and motorcycles and a pedestrian path that cuts under the bridge and allows direct access to the river for washing, cleaning, or fishing. The aim is for the bridge to become a social hub for the village,

providing steps for seating, shaded areas for relaxation, and a meeting point. The folded ribbon also creates a diversity of spaces and allows the landscape and river to be experienced from different perspectives. The bridge is constructed from cast-concrete that is dyed with black pigment to distinguish itself from the typical grey concrete of the highway viaduct that hovers high above it.

Despite its small scale this bridge facilitates a critical link for the local village economy that is simply overlooked by more top-down planning methods. As distinct nodes, the series of bridge designs explores the possibility for architecture at a micro-scale to interact with infrastructure at a completely opposite scale. The conflict of scales is central to the many issues, economical, social, and spatial, that afflict villages today.

← pp. 66/67: Villagers use the bridge to access the riverbed for washing clothes.

↓ Different views of the bridge

Taiping Village

BRIDGING THE PAST

A project to renovate a three hundred-year-old Tang Dynasty bridge in Guizhou Province goes beyond the design of the physical bridge and engages the social, economic, and cultural issues concerning the village itself.
The design process began with the problem of a collapsed arch—to repair the connection between two sides of a river—but expanded to encompass the larger issue of historical connection between the past and the present condition of the village. This process also involved bridging between traditional and modern techniques, both of which were deployed in the final design.
The project necessitated the collaboration between NGOs from Hong Kong and China, local government, schools of architecture, students, and villagers. The final result is still simply a bridge. But in the two-year process of design and construction, the bridge takes on both a literal and symbolic meaning.

↘ View of Taiping
Bridge in 2006 with
a collapsed arch

A   The bridge was first built in Qing Dynasty in the 1700s.

B   An arch bridge was built in the 1900s.

C   The bridge was rebuilt with multiple arches in the 1950s.

D   In the summer of 2005 an arch of the bridge collapsed under heavy rainfall and flooding.

E   Scaffolding is constructed during a two-month dry season.

F   The arch is rebuilt with pre-cast concrete blocks.

G   The bridge face is rebuilt with stones recovered from the bridge collapse.

H   A new waterproofing layer is applied.

I   The bridge is paved with custom designed concrete pavers to provide seating and planting areas.

J   The planting of the bridge is conducted with student volunteers and villagers together.

Bridging the River

In 2005, one arch of the masonry bridge collapsed because of flooding. The following year a team of students and teachers from the University of Hong Kong and Chongqing University visited the bridge for the first time. The project was initially defined as the repair of the broken arch. However, after the site investigation, a historical plaque was unearthed that described the long history of the bridge. Over its three-hundred-year history the bridge had been renovated, repaired, and altered many times. This was simply another stage in its historical development. The bridge surface at the time had eroded into a dilapidated state. We decided to preserve the bridge and also renovate its surface.

The reason for the disrepair of the bridge was due to recent changes in the dynamics of the village. Historically, this bridge was the most important connection between two neighboring villages. It was also the site of the weekly marketplace. However, the construction of a new highway bypassed the bridge. This caused a shift of focus away from the river as the main infrastructure and commercial center. Five hundred meters away, along the new highway, dozens of new shops have opened up hoping to take advantage of the increased car traffic. The real challenge was how to preserve the importance of the bridge as a significant place: as a locus for village activities as it had been in the past. We intended to enable this revitalization by inserting a very different, contemporary surface to create this new public space.

↓ The local market is held on the riverbank while the bridge is under repair

↘ New commercial opportunities along the highway

Bridging Techniques

The initial idea was to fix the masonry bridge using traditional techniques. However after interviewing the villagers, we concluded there was no longer the expertise necessary to hand-cut stone for the arch. Instead a team of students from Chongqing University working under Dr. Xing, a professor of engineering, came up with a plan to precast concrete blocks in a nearby factory and still lay the arch in the traditional manner. The most complicated part of the process was building the bridge scaffolding with local craftsmen and materials during a two-week window when the river level was at its lowest. The stone blocks from the collapsed arch were recycled into the cladding of the new arch.

← A timber scaffold construction before the arch repair

↓ Students discussing with villagers

↙ Precast concrete blocks for the arch

↗ The process of making new triangular pavers out of PVC pipes in a local factory

Working with the same local factory, a new system of precast concrete pavers was designed that would program the bridge in different ways. Inspired by the variety and widespread use of open pavers in China, a new typology of pavers was prototyped in the factory. These pavers come in different sizes and have varying sizes of openings. A triangular geometry was employed in order to facilitate the combination of different size modules. PVC pipe was a simple and cost efficient way to create the formwork for the openings. Cast as voids and solids, the collection of pavers makes a transition from hard-walking surface to planters and to seating.

Bridging Communities

↗ Students helping
to plant the bridge

↑ Paving the bridge

← Planting the bridge

Rather than hiring contractors, students and villagers worked together over a two-week period to move and position the pavers. The planting was done by sourcing local vegetation directly from the neighboring hillside. Villagers were also eager to donate plants directly from their gardens. Despite the straightforward nature of the physical project, there were no institutionalized pathways for funding and implementing a project of this nature. From start to finish, the project was fundamentally about organizing a network of

collaborations. After the project was completed we submitted the project to the UNESCO Asia-Pacific Awards for Cultural Heritage Conservation, as an example of working in a historic, rural village. The jury expressed "strong reservations about the insertion of new materials and the application of designs and techniques that were not fully in keeping with the bridge's original character." We came to realize the fine line between preservation and renovation. In this project we had to look beyond the bridge itself to understand the larger dynamic occurring in the village and its surroundings. It is difficult to identify what the "original character" of the bridge is, considering it has been renovated and adapted many times over the past three hundred years. After the renovation, the bridge site further evolved and became more relevant because of the construction of a nearby middle school that meant students frequently used the bridge before and after classes.

Against the overwhelming destruction of heritage in China, especially in remote rural areas, the issue of preservation is of critical importance. As villages in China undergo rapid and dynamic changes, the question is whether it is possible to balance a sense of history with a clear sense of forward looking development. By understanding the current changes in relation to the past, architectural interventions can act to preserve continuity between past and present, while anticipating future transformation.

← pp. 76/77: The completed bridge showing pavers and planters

↓ Local school kids using the bridge

Suburban Village

RISE OF THE MIDDLE CLASS

A profound effect of China's restructured economy is that some people have become very rich. As people become wealthier they desire changes to their lifestyle: their clothes, material goods, habits, and where and how they choose to live. Housing in China is now something one can select, a commodity that stratifies income levels and social groups. The massive overhaul of housing policy was one step behind the successive policy changes regarding economy and land use. Tantamount to Thatcher's neo-liberal and extremely controversial "Right-to-buy" scheme of the 1980s (Deng and Thatcher met in 1982), China set about to privatize its public housing stock incrementally to create a commercially driven housing market. Without going into detail about those reforms here, the result was that by 1999 the financial tools (mortgages, loans) and conjugation of land use rights with property rights had been institutionalized to propel the real estate market and encourage the buying and selling of houses. By 2000 the majority of public sector housing across cities in China had been absorbed into private ownership.[1] This has led to a massive construction boom and with it a plethora of housing choices for different income levels and tastes. The emerging middle class and financially well-off have driven this production in different typologies of development. Real estate enclaves, secured tower compounds, themed villas, and gated communities, all now proliferate in the urban landscape of China.[2] This influx of residential development has also been coupled with consumption landscapes of theme-parks, shopping malls, and golf courses. In some instances these are conjoined and crossed to form permutations of imagineered shopping malls, golf course towers, and gated enclaves designed as simulations of historic architectural styles. These recombinants of what Sorkin describes as "variations on a theme park" now infiltrate not only the major conurbations but are enacted in almost every emerging urbanized region in China.[3] Although the much flaunted and criticized themed satellite towns of Shanghai, such as Thames Town (Songjiang) or German Town (Anting), are extreme examples of thematization and its discontents, what is perhaps less discussed is the pervasive production of thematized typologies as a normative mode of housing construction.[4]

1   Song, Yan, Gerrit Knapp, and Chengri Ding. 2005. "Housing Policy in the People's Republic of China: An Historical Review." In Chengri Ding and Yan Song, eds. *Emerging Land and Housing Markets in China*. pp. 163–182. Lincoln Institute of Land Policy, Cambridge, Massachusetts

2   Campanella, Thomas J. 2008. "Theme Parks and the Landscape of Consumption." In *The Concrete Dragon: China's Urban Revolution and What It Means for the World*. Princeton Architectural Press, New York

3   Sorkin, Michael. 1992. "See You in Disneyland." In Michael Sorkin, ed. *Variations on a Theme Park: The new American city and the end of public space.*, Hill and Wang, New York

4   Choon-Piew, Pow. 2009. *Gated Communities in China: Class, Privilege and the Moral Politics of the Good Life*. Routledge, London, New York

Many similar examples in the United States are usually attributed to out-of-town or suburban development; however, in urbanized areas such as Shenzhen and Dongguan in Guangdong province, the clear separation of urban center and suburb is not so delineated. Instead, these types of suburban developments exist as bounded enclaves within the urban fabric of the city. For example, in Shenzhen, adjacent to Shennan Boulevard—its major east-west axis—a residential tower is integrated with a golf course, with apartments with golf-course-views sold at a premium price.

Dongguan emerged as a competitor and potential successor to Shenzhen for manufacturing industries. Like Shenzhen this model of urbanization related to industrial processes was rapid, with villages playing an active role as entrepreneurial agents in the transformation of rural land into factories and housing for migrant workers. As individuals and companies prospered, the housing market evolved and became more established according to the policy changes outlined above. By 2000, villages in Dongguan were not only focusing on rural to industrial transformation but were also selling their land rights or leasing their farm land to developers investing in leisure landscapes or residential enclaves.

↓ Batou, 2009

↘ Batou, 2011

Wanjiang District on the edge of Dongguan's designated urban center reveals two examples of how villages adapted to this new market. As villages were annexed into this urban territory, village committees saw opportunities to develop village land. Batou Village Committee, acting as a stakeholder management company, leased the collective land of the village to a developer. In a patch approximately 700 × 300 m and edged by an urban village, a river, and a highway, the developer constructed over twelve residential slab blocks, 60 m long and over 20 stories high, all orientated in an east-west direction. In return for their land-lease the villagers received two forms of compensation: an apartment unit was promised to each family in the new residential blocks and the village committee distributed a share of the rental fee, roughly 200 RMB per month.[5] This development contrasts with the last remaining plot of village land, just across the development on the other side of the street. This residual patch of agricultural land is still farmed by the villagers for bananas, water spinach, and strawberries; however, as they now have an alternative income, it is mainly used for leisure purposes. Inevitably the land will be developed but as village corporations have become more financially savvy they would rather play a waiting game with developers for the most lucrative deal.

Just 1.5 km away, still within Wanjiang district, a different story of middle-class development has unfolded. Alex Hu, a local instant noodle magnate, envisaged the creation of the world's biggest shopping mall, built essentially in the middle of nowhere. Working closely with the local government, who supported the project through developing road infrastructure and

5 Interview with villagers, 2008

↱ pp. 82/83: New South China Mall with themed elements highlighted

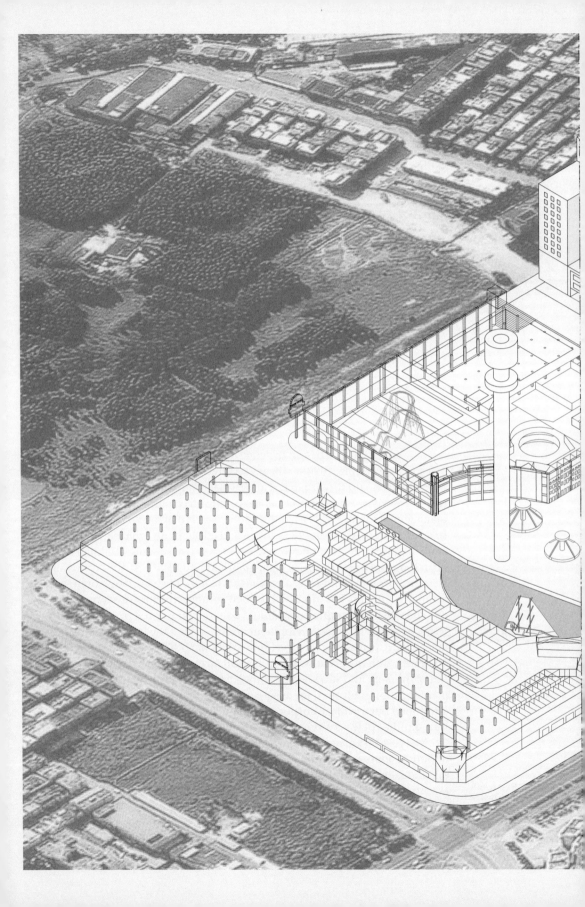

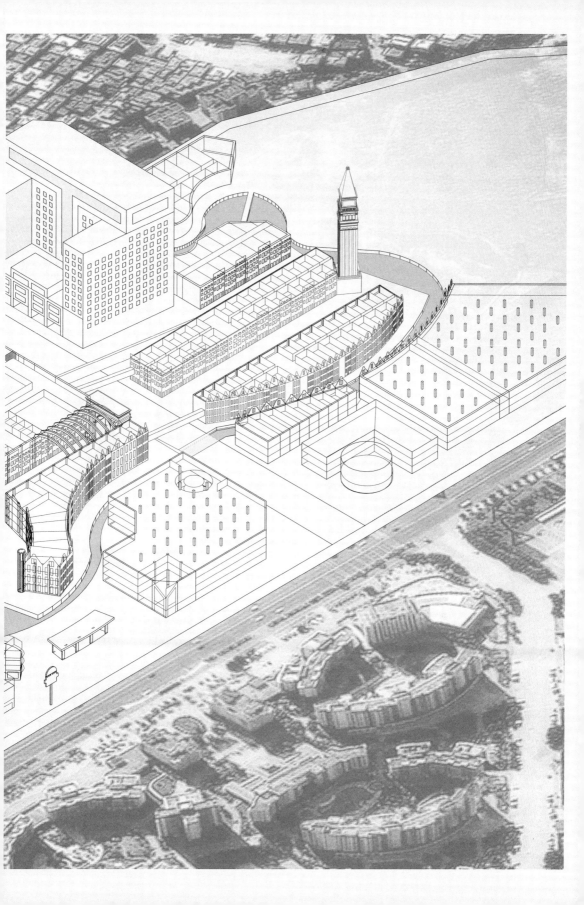

a bus terminus, land was collected from local villages and construction began in 2003. The design combined representational built elements—the Venetian Campanile, a partial facade of the Doges Palace, a canal with gondolas, an Arc de Triomphe whose roof extended into an extruded space-frame galleria, Dutch gabled shop fronts—together with masses of retail space. Added to this mix, there is an amusement park (Amazing World) with rides and indoor roller coaster, an aquarium, a cinema, and the mall is populated by roving Teletubby-suited staff aimed at encouraging you to spend more. Unfortunately since construction was completed in 2005 the mall's retail space has remained 99% vacant. Despite a change of management and the completion of Phase Two of the mall in 2011, a recent visit in 2013 found the mall's retail space still predominantly empty.

    Perhaps the scale of the mall was premature for its middle-class catchment or the middle-class simply is not consuming quite as much as anticipated? In the future it is possible that the mall will be a success, and to a certain extent it is unlikely that the local government would ever let it fail completely. If anything there are signs that they seem to be actively promoting the construction of housing around the mall, with a new patch of villa housing developed at its southern edge in 2013.

    These two examples describe suburban typologies that have evolved from the transformation of rural village land. They represent the ensuing proliferation of these enclaves within the urban fabric of Chinese cities. Unlike the dispersed sprawl of single family house typologies found throughout the West, the development of this suburban fabric reads as a carpet of individuated patches, some with high density towers, slab blocks, and other typologies not usually associated with the suburbs. To this extent Soja's definition of the "Exopolis"— his description of the urbanization of peripheral cities in Los Angeles—seems a more appropriate description: "the city without" having the dual, contradictory qualities of "city-full non-city-ness."[6] He uses the example of Orange County, California, autonomous and detached from Los Angeles, to describe an ambiguous urban territory that operates differently from suburbia or the center. The ingredients and "scenes" that compose Soja's reading of Orange County are of course different from those in Shenzhen and Dongguan. However, the similarity of spatial products—theme parks, malls, community enclaves—allude to an evolving spatial geography of suburban China that has more in common with the edge cities of Los Angeles than we may have originally anticipated.

← pp. 84/85: Abandoned suburban development

↑ Entire sections of the mall are empty

↖ Teletubby Land

6 Soja, Edward W. 1991. "Inside Exopolis: Scenes from Orange County." In Michael Sorkin, ed. *Variations on a Theme Park: The New American City and the End of Public Space*. Hill and Wang, New York

Yanzhou Village

ISLAND URBANISM

↗ Model showing design interventions

Yanzhou village is a small island in a Pearl River tributary running through the Pearl River Delta (PRD) near the city of Zhaoqing and just one hour west of Guangzhou. We were commissioned by a developer to transform the island into a new recreational destination for the rising middle classes in the region. The developer was an aspiring local company that had been building malls and housing in Zhaoqing (one of nine prefectures in the PRD). Typical of many other second and third tier cities in China, this city of half a million inhabitants had become the refuge for middle-class residents of nearby Guangzhou. In the city of Guangzhou with a total population of over 12 million, nearly 35% is considered middle class (those making 12,000 to 30,000 RMB per year). The number continues to grow, having doubled over the past ten years. The brief was open ended without any fixed program: we were asked to transform this rural village island into a middle-class leisure isle—an escape and sanctuary from the big city.

The deal between the developer and the villagers was a ten-year lease on the entire island. Through this process, the villagers also hoped to become "middle-class" citizens, not only from the income of the lease agreement but also through their own investments in potential house rentals, restaurants, and shops. Currently, the island remains relatively empty with large areas of old houses, banana plantations, and fishponds. As the island is accessible only by boat, it remains an oasis of under-development in an otherwise fast growing town. Our approach was to see if we could preserve the existing remote, rural quality of the island. We proposed to insert programs as concentrated "islands" in the existing fabric, linked together by a bicycle and pedestrian boardwalk as a form of island urbanism. This would minimize impact on the environment as well as maximizing the island experience.

← pp. 88/89: View toward the island and the existing ferry pier

Inspired by the *tulous* in Fujian Province, which are essentially an urban typology in the midst of the rural, our islands are circles of various sizes containing different programs. Some are simple sport courts while others like the spa island are filled with small pools and programs. We even designed a system of floating recreational islands connected by a boardwalk. Utilizing the fishponds in the center of the island, the island is surrounded by water inside and out. Cultivating the planting and landscape strategy to intensify the notion of seasonal and tidal changes, we envisioned the island experience to be the opposite of city life.

After the preliminary presentation, we came back to find that our design had already been rendered into gigantic billboard advertisements. Our design was now a luxury island of big sailboats, even containing an airport for private planes. After a few more meetings where we made analysis on capacity and potential earnings, the developers informed us that they would no longer go ahead with the project. Apparently, they had planned all along to sub-lease the island to yet another developers. Our design proposal had helped to "sell" the idea of the island's potential. Unfortunately we never heard from them again. We were never even paid our final contract sum. To this day, the island remains quiet and remote.

↖ The interior of the island

Contested Village

EVOLVING SPATIAL GEOGRAPHIES

As the dynamics of thirty years of untrammeled urbanization evolve, disputes over land rights, compensation and development control are escalating in China. Most contested issues remain at a local level and go unreported, however, as in the case of Wukan, in Guangdong Province, the village uprising and the government's reaction became the focus of national, and then international, media. Rather than focus on these high-profile disputed sites, which have been subject to extensive coverage, this article takes an unknown, but archetypal, contested piece of village land in Jian Sha Zhou on the periphery of Dongguan in Southern China as its central case study. The village territory combines residual islands of stasis alongside areas of rapid residential development and industrial productivity. This article explores the evolving spatial geographies of the village and its unique spatial contrasts that exhibit the competing and contradictory forces acting upon it. The case study exemplifies the robust adaptability of villages that have emerged from simple agricultural units into multi-differentiated economic agents. It also identifies intrinsic problems in this process that will shape the future development of these volatile sites.

Contested Territory

In 2008 on an excursion from Shenzhen to Guangzhou exploring the effects of the economic global downturn in urban areas in the Pearl River Delta in Southern China, we visited Jian Sha Zhou, a village of 1,800 people on the outskirts of Dongguan. In January 2009, Fiona Tam's article "Laid-off migrants doomed to suffer in crisis" in *The South China Morning Post*, reported that up to 20 million migrant workers across the PRD had vacated their factory dormitories and returned to their village homes. In anticipation we were expecting to find peripheral urban areas dormant and development ceased. A plot of land in Jian Sha Zhou seemed to provide us with the evidence we needed: a scattering of three- to four- story brick houses were unfinished without windows or any external cladding. In addition the buildings had no clothes drying outside the windows indicating that the houses

were unoccupied. The buildings appeared as isolated blocks situated in an agricultural landscape of vegetable patches and banana trees. This built fabric was very different from the typical village typology found in Southern China of dense clusters of village houses surrounded by fields and planting areas. At first glance the visual evidence seemed to support that this indeed was a half-finished construction that had been curtailed by the financial crisis and that the migrant workers had simply returned home. Three years later in 2011 we revisited this site to find out what had changed. Our assumption was that we would find this land fully developed without any traces of its rural origins as the economic climate in China had resumed its vigor. Remarkably the plot remained unchanged, yet at its edge two new residential towers of over thirty stories had been constructed and the village hummed with industrial activity. How could such rapid development co-exist with such vacancy? Why did this one plot of land remain untouched and undeveloped, yet the village itself seemed rampant with new construction and economic fervor? This article investigates the evolving spatial geographies of this village as a microcosm of the impact of rural urbanization and associated political context. Rather than focus on land market policy, property rights, or the precise legal frameworks of Chinese land development,[1] the research focuses on the spatial implications of the urban transformation process. As a mini-scenario, this case-study highlights prototypical urban conditions that reveal clues to the forces and possible effects that might mold China's urban future.[2]

1   See: Ho, Samuel P. S., and George C. S. Lin. 2003. "Emerging Land Markets in Rural and Urban China: Policies and Practices." In *The China Quarterly*, No. 175 (Sep. 2003) pp. 681–707; and Ho, Peter. 2001. "Who Owns China's Land? Policies, Property Rights and Deliberate Institutional Ambiguity." In *The China Quarterly*, No. 166 (June 2001), pp. 394–421

2   *Mini-scenarios—experiential moments within the city—as described by Raoul Bunschoten can reflect and provide insights as microcosms of larger urban flows: Bunschoten, Raoul, Hélène Binet, and Takuro Hoshino. 2001. *Urban Flotsam: Stirring the City: Chora*. Rotterdam: 010 Publishers

← pp. 92/93: Jian Sha Zhou: the half completed buildings on the Danwei site 2008

→ Patchwork urbanism: the example of Dongguan, © 2011 Google and © DigitalGlobe 2012

↙ Before and after: Jian Sha Zhou in 2008 and 2011 showing the development of residential towers versus the stasis of the contested ground.

3 For an overview of China's historical evolution see: Spence, Jonathan D. 1999. *The Search for Modern China*, W. W. Norton & Company, New York, London

4 Shane, Grahame. 2006. "The Emergence of Landscape Urbanism." In *The Landscape Urbanism Reader*, edited by Charles Waldheim, pp. 55–57. New York, Princeton Architectural Press

5 Fan, Cindy. 1995. "Of Belts and Ladders: State Policy and Uneven Regional Development in Post-Mao China." *Annals of the Association of American Geographers*, Vol. 85, No. 3 (Sep. 1995), pp. 421–449

6 Ho, Samuel P. S., and C. S. George. 2004. "Non-Agricultural Land Use in Post-Reform China." *The China Quarterly*, No.179 (Sep. 2004), pp. 758–781

A Territory in Transition

The volatile conditions of land transformation from rural to urban over the last thirty years in China has created territories of uncertain status. Nowhere is this more pronounced than in Guangdong Province in the Pearl River Delta, (PRD). As a pioneer province of China's opening up, enabled through the formation of specialized economic enclaves,[3] a predominantly agricultural landscape has mutated into what Cedric Price has described as a "scrambled egg" of urban substance. Price described the modern city as a scrambled egg whereby the center and periphery are no longer distinct but have become interlaced and indistinguishable from each other.[4] This blurred condition between edge and periphery is pronounced and extensive in the PRD. However on closer inspection this scrambled substance consists of a patchwork of distinct territories in different stages of transformation: golf courses, suburban housing, villages, agricultural land, factories, construction sites, and abandoned projects all co-exist within this urban carpet. Uneven development occurs at a regional scale,[5] a provincial scale,[6] and also at the scale of land plots. These patches develop at different speeds depending on the power, financial status, and political clout of individuals and agencies acting on this terrain.

One distinguishing factor and one that has been a determining factor in how land has developed in China is the lack of clarity of land ownership rights. This impacts government infrastructural projects, developer driven housing, and projects undertaken by influential village co-operatives or by individual entrepreneurs alike. In some instances the complex issues surrounding land ownership rights and those staking a claim to these rights result in conflict.[7] In these examples these patches reach stasis leaving fallow land: ruins, demolition sites, or half-completed buildings. This land is caught in a stalemate exhibiting the results of conflicting forces played out among the different agents in the urbanization process. In this sense they are anomalies—islands of uncertain status, neither fully rural nor urbanized—that are surrounded by pervasive territorial transformation.

Post-Mao, economic reforms necessitated the evolution of laws regarding land ownership and land use in order to ease development and stimulate market forces. The earliest mechanisms were triggered in rural areas. In 1981 villagers became able to lease their land as long as the original ownership remained the same.[8] In 1982 the constitution divided land into urban land that was designated as state owned and rural land that was owned by the village collective and instituted a legal structure allowing rural land to be changed to state land via expropriation.[9] As industrialization fuelled the need for expansion of urban areas, this infringement on the rural necessitated the conversion of rural land to urban land. This transition is made through "expropriation," deemed to be in the greater public interest, with villagers being compensated for their land and their loss of income. In 1988 the law changed to allow land not only to shift from rural to urban, but also to allow land use rights to be sold or leased at market value.[10]

The escalating speed of development that these policies catalyzed brought with it unforeseen situations and disputes, and as a result the legal system had to adapt to try to keep pace. Even though the language of Chinese land law is often straightforward, the degree to which it is interpreted, executed, or monitored vastly varies between provinces, local city governance, and village collectives.[11] The wide margin between law and its practice has created the potential for black-market loopholes or grey areas to emerge in this space of obfuscation.[12] The opportunities created by such loopholes have allowed land to develop into unanticipated uses and haphazard organizations based on unbridled profiteering. The also increases the possibility of contestation among stakeholders including villagers, local governments, developers, or factory owners that surfaces through the ambiguity of development rights, land compensation, and the designation of rural or urban land.[13]

Village Adaptation and Evolution

For many rural villages within the fast growing hinterland of the Pearl River Delta these new legal constructs provided incentives to shift from a purely agrarian community to one that engaged with real estate development and management, factory construction, or industrial production. The staggering adaptability of the villagers to engage in a diverse range of economic activities is overseen through the village co-operative: in essence the village management company. Operating as an executive board of a large corporation the village co-operative manages the economic decisions of its shareholders (the villagers), social welfare services, and municipal services. A twin organization, the village committee, often with the same members, mediates between the higher level

7 Guo, Xiaolin. 2001. "Land Expropriation and Rural Conflicts in China." *The China Quarterly*, No. 166 (Jun. 2001), pp. 422–439

8 Xinhua News Agency. 1991. "Minutes of National Rural Work," promulgated by Central Committee of Communist Party of China. Accessed August 2011. http://news.xinhuanet.com/politics/2008-10/08/content_10162735.html (site discontinued)

9 China Law Edu. 1982. "Constitution of People's Republic of China," promulgated by National People's Congress of People's Republic of China. *China Law Edu.* Accessed August 2011. http://www.chinalawedu.com/falvfagui/fg21752/10928.shtml

10 Constitutional Amendment of People's Republic of China, promulgated by National People's Congress of People's Republic of China 1988. *Lawyee.* Accessed August 2011. http://www.lawyee.org/Act/Act_Display.asp?ChannelID=1010100&RID=27837&KeyWord=1988+%E5%AE%AA%E6%B3%95

11 Ho, Peter. 2001. "Who Owns China's Land? Policies, Property Rights and Deliberate Institutional Ambiguity." *The China Quarterly*, No. 166 (Jun. 2001), pp. 394–421

12 Lin, George C. S. 2009. "The Evolving Land System and Land Markets." In *Developing China: Land, Politics and Social Conditions*, New York, Routledge

13 Cai, Yongshun. 2003. "Collective Ownership or Cadres' Ownership? The Non-Agricultural Use of Farmland in China." *The China Quarterly*, No. 175 (Sep. 2003), pp. 662–680

local government and the village and is responsible for administering policies at a local level. Interestingly, these leaders are democratically elected by the villagers themselves although more often than not, the appointed Communist Party cadre is the most successful candidate.

In some cases the relationship between the village chief and the villagers themselves can become fractious, particularly if the chief is seen to be favoring the priorities of the local government over the needs of the village or is undertaking corrupt practices. This is most acute when it comes to land sales. The recent example of Wukan in the PRD in December 2011 demonstrated the escalation from discontent about land sales to a full blown protest. In that case the village chief was accused by villagers of expropriating land without due compensation to the villagers. Given that local governments acquire almost one third of their revenue from land sales, there are clear incentives to sell village land.[14] The protest was amplified after one village protester, Xue Jinbo, died in police custody apparently from a "sudden illness." Owing to the mass media coverage both locally and internationally,[15] the local government unusually met the villagers' demands. The village head was replaced with the leader of the demonstrations, two local government officials were fired, and an investigation into the death of Xue Jinbo was promised. Yet this example is only one of potentially hundreds of thousands of protests that occur each year.[16] Exact data are impossible to find because of their sensitive nature, with any official government figures presumed to be massively underestimated.[17]

The change in policy in 1988 to allow land rights to be leased or sold has been a driver for these increasing numbers of disputes. No longer simply an issue between villagers and local governments the shift toward land as an increasingly profitable commodity has extended and diversified the set of potential stakeholders to real estate developers, foreign companies, business entrepreneurs, or even other wealthier village co-operatives.

The evolution and adaptation of the village co-operative is exemplified by Yu Min Cun village, a simple fishing village prior to 1978, situated directly on the border between Hong Kong and Shenzhen. Because of its strategic location adjacent to the financial powerhouse of Hong Kong, with close family networks that extended across the border, economic development occurred rapidly and smoothly. This was also true for companies and individuals investing from Taiwan and other overseas Chinese who utilized Hong Kong as a mediator and entry conduit into the mainland. As the first wave of development left some villages increasingly wealthy, some village co-operatives diversified their investment portfolios to include investing in other villages in other parts of the PRD. In the 1980s, Yu Min Cun had profited from expropriating its land to the local government and to Hong Kong investors wishing to set up factories. In the next phase in the 1990s, the village corporation (as a result of the 1988 legislation), bought the land use rights to a 3,000 m^2 plot of land over 60 km away in Dongguan. Since Dongguan was emerging as the next industrialized landscape with attractive economic incentives set in place by the city government, this was a shrewd move and highlights the inter-connected capacity for growth that is embedded within the social and familial networks found in the PRD.[18]

Under the auspices of control and hierarchical organization the evolution of economic policy during the 1980s in effect triggered multiple ways by individuals, companies, or villages to make money. Once unleashed,

14 Bristow, Michael. "Wukan unrest: Why Do Chinese Farmers Riot?" *BBC News.* 15 December 2011. Accessed August 2011. http://www.bbc.co.uk/news/world-asia-china-16193089

15 For example: BBC News."Chinese Revolt Leader becomes Village Chief of Wukan." 16 January 2012. Accessed August 2011. http://www.bbc.co.uk/news/world-asia-china-16571568

16 Li, Lianjiang, and Kevin J. O'Brien. 1996. "Villagers and Popular Resistance in Contemporary China," *Modern China,* Vol. 22, No. 1 (Jan. 1996), pp. 28–61

17 Bristow, M. 2011

18 Smart, J., and A. Smart. 1991. "Personal Connections and Divergent Economies: A Case Study of Hong Kong Investment in China." In *International Journal of Urban and Regional Research* 15, 2: pp. 216–233

further incentives to cut corners, reduce administration fees, and raise profit margins were realized through loopholes in the system or corrupt practices.[19] These include villagers selling or leasing their homes for commercial uses; state owned enterprises selling their land use rights at market value without paying money to the local government; the village collective exchanging land rights for developer shareholdings; or local governments expropriating land from villages without due compensation. All these mechanisms set the stage for potential conflicts, disagreements, and widespread profiteering.

19 Lin, George, 2009

Speed versus Stasis

The contextual background and macro-policies described above serve as a basis for understanding the mechanisms of transformation occurring in Jian Sha Zhou. By conducting interviews with local residents, factory owners, and the local village committee between June and August 2011 the impact of these large scale policies and resultant local contestation was pieced together as a case-study documenting the process of rural to urban transformation.[20] Three small agricultural villages that had produced rice and fish under three production teams during collectivization, were joined under one village committee after 1978. In the 1980s the committee was encouraged by the local government to develop the industrial production of fireworks and bricks. This failed and the committee switched from direct investment to management. To raise capital, some of the land-use rights were sold to outside investors and the money used to build factories. These were leased to foreign companies that were attracted to the cheaper rents and cheaper labor costs compared to the more established factory areas of Shenzhen, as well as the natural resources such as the river.

The first factory was a print-works operated by a Hong Kong investor that was soon followed by a garment factory by a Taiwanese company. These

20 A series of interviews were conducted in Jian Sha Zhou between June and August 2011 by the Author, Liang Zhiyong, Timo Heinonen, and Tian Xuezhu. All interviews were conducted either in Putonghua or Guandonghua and translated into English by Liang Zhiyong. Where names are not shown, anonymity was preferred by the interviewee.

↙ Jian Sha Zhou under transformation, © 2013 Google and © DigitalGlobe 2013

← pp. 98/99: Jian Sha Zhou's emerging urban fabric

examples stimulated local entrepreneurs to engage in industrialization, such as the Dongguan Baojian Paper Company—a paper factory that gained a preferential land lease from the village collective in 1989.

At the same time that the village began undertaking the shift from agricultural production to management and industrial production, a plot of land was acquired by a former Danwei (Dongguan Electrochemical Group)—an industrial production unit under collectivization—which decided to use the land to build houses for its workers. The shift away from the Danwei system to state owned enterprises post-1978 left many of these entities in financial disarray. As a result the company decided to divide up the land-rights-use and sublet this to its employees or other non-locals for housing construction. This is an illegal action—the state company had no legal authority to approve the occupation of the land.[21] Shortly after the construction of these three-story houses began in the early 1990s, the local government prevented any further construction on the site, much to the chagrin of the occupiers:

21 Ho, Lin, 2003

> Joshua Bolchover: Why has construction been suspended?
> Local Resident: I don't know. Go ask the village officials. ...It is absolutely absurd! We acquired the land through due process and have all the certificates, how can they do that? It's no use talking about law with the party. They just do what they want.

In 1993 the Dongguan government built a new highway directly adjacent to the plot, subsuming the land within a new planning status, that of urban greenery, thus rendering any new construction illegal. As a result the houses have remained in a half-finished state for almost twenty years—an astonishing fact for a region that has, according to the United Nations, one of the fastest rates of urbanization in the world.[22]

22 United Nations Department of Economic and Social Affairs, Population Division. "World Urbanization Prospects: The 2011 Revision.": 8. Accessed 18 June 2012. http://esa.un.org/unpd/wup/pdf/WUP2011_ighlights.pdf

Since our first visit in 2008 the majority of blocks still remain empty, however a small number are occupied with migrant workers who lease the buildings from the resident owners and have moved to the town to work in the local factories. The residual land around the blocks is planted with vegetable patches of corn, beans, and choi sum, which are tended to by these inhabitants. The resultant urban fabric manifests the stalemate between the owners of the blocks and the village officials. Both are playing a waiting game to see who will succumb first. The critical and contentious point is regarding the actual nature of the acquisition of the land. In the eyes of the owners, they believe that the land was expropriated by the Danwei and therefore converted from rural to urban land and that they were given permission to build their houses. If that were the case the village collective would have no rights to this land. The Deputy Secretary of Jian Sha Zhou Village Committee, Mr. Liu Zufa, of course argues the opposite—that the land is theirs:

> Mr. Liu Zufa: Say whatever they want! At the end of the day, it's rural land and it belongs to the collective.

Whatever agreements were made and contracts signed the original documents, according to Mr. Liu Zufa, cannot be found. Even if they were to be recovered, it is unclear whether their validity would remain or be overruled by the new planning policies that zone the area as urban greenway, prohibiting any form of construction. The officials at the time have also long been replaced and so the stasis continues.

↙ The adaptation of
the shop-house

↘ The contested Danwei
site and new highway,
image

Yet this stasis on this plot is in stark contrast to the development of the
surrounding village, which has witnessed rapid industrialization and
construction. The success of the Baojian Paper Company was paralleled by
changes in Chinese consumer habits: according to one paper factory's data,
from 1990 to 2003 toilet paper consumption increased 11% every year,
providing an increasingly profitable industrial sector.[23] This quickly spawned
an industrial network of different sized companies: Baojian processed raw
pulp from Guangxi into paper and cardboard tubes; other companies
produced plastic wrapping; and small scale family businesses processed the
large rolls into small rolls and packaged them ready for distribution. This
attracted businesses from elsewhere: from Sichuan, Zhejiang, and Shanghai.
The village collective also invested and is currently responsible for 30%
of all factories. As the demand for factories increased so has the rent. Ms. Lu,
a paper workshop owner, and Ms. Ye, a manager of a paper factory, explained
that rents had increased up to 60% in just three years from 2008 to 2011.
As a result many villagers shifted from production to land management,
building factories for rent or leasing their land to these newcomer operations
via the 1988 legislation allowing them to lease or sell their rights to land use
as long as they had permission from the village committee.

> When one walks around Jian Sha Zhou, the transformation of this
village into a distributed factory network for toilet paper is self-evident. Large
two-meter long rolls of paper are hauled from factories to domestic production
houses. These buildings are adaptations of the typical village shop-house. This
typology consists of a ground floor commercial shop front with an overhanging
second and third story for living. In this case the shop is replaced by a small
assembly room: typically, a large table full of toilet rolls being placed into
wrappers by four to six people sitting on plastic chairs with a band-saw in the
back to cut the large rolls into smaller units. The floor above is used for storage
with the windows extended into a large floor-to-ceiling opening to winch
materials into, or out of, the room and into a waiting truck. Accommodation

23 Zhongshan City Xiaolan
Town Yuan Xiang Paper
Products Factory.
"In the next 10 years:
China's tissue paper
industry golden period
of development."
10 March 2008.
Accessed 25 August
2011. http://www.aeos
.cn/En/Info/Html/2008-
7/Info_6_20902312
.html

is located on the uppermost floors. Together this network of small-to medium-to large-scale producers, each with a differentiated role to contribute, collectively can, as claimed by Ms. Ye, manager of the paper factory, earn yearly returns of several billion renmenbi with current trade extending as far afield as Africa.

↖ The distributed factory of toilet roll production

This transformation of the village into an industrial production network has accumulated capital for the village collective and made some villagers wealthy. Although some villagers are directly involved in the production process, the majority of workers and business operators are outsiders. The local villagers, for the most part, are indirectly involved as land agents or are responsible for constructing and leasing factory buildings.

In contrast to the industrial evolution of the village, the other most radical change in the two years since we visited the site was the construction of three new residential towers of around twenty stories that overlooked the contested Danwei site. This block of residential development is typologically more attributed to areas closer to urban districts rather than industrial peripheral areas as described by Jian Sha Zhou. What was the motivation for this construction, who were the stakeholders, and why had this construction taken place so quickly?

The Village No More

24 Dongguan Government.
    "Guiding Suggestions
    on Some Issues of
    Dongguan 'Villager to
    Resident' Work." 2004.
    Accessed August 2011.
    http://www.law110.com/
    law/city/dongguan/
    200464006.html

In 2004 Dongguan City Government launched its "villagers to residents" policy.[24] This mechanism was introduced to make expropriation of land easier: to free up land that was owned by the villagers, particularly land that was occupied by village houses, for industrial or higher density residential use. The policy was implemented based on a set of criteria that effectively judged whether the village was still rural or had become urban in character. The Dongguan government issued the following guidelines in 2004 and if the village met just one of the following conditions it was deemed eligible to become a "shequ" or urban neighborhood: If more than 50% of the population had an urban hukou; if there was less than 80m^2 of farmland per capita; or more than two thirds of villagers were no longer involved in agricultural production. Clearly for any of the rural villages that had undergone industrialization any of these conditions were typical rather than exceptional. The effect of becoming a shequ meant that all villagers received an urban hukou and so became eligible for social services such as health care and education. However, their collective land became state land, albeit with compensation, effectively transforming rural land into urban land and placing the control of the land within the state apparatus.

In terms of organization, the village committee effectively remained the same. It was renamed as a resident committee with the villagers becoming residents with shareholdings in all village enterprises. Fundamentally this shifts the balance away from villagers as entrepreneurs toward the village co-operative as the predominant agent of change. Furthermore land itself has become more of an asset, an abstract financial tool made up of numerous

↘ Jian Sha Zhou,
    A new *shequ*

↑ The rampant
construction of
residential towers
in Dongguan as part
of China's overheated
housing bubble

← Model of new residential
development:
a business venture
between the village
co-operative and
a private developer

→ Batou's fragmented
landscape of farmland
and new residential
construction, 2009

shareholders rather than a substance that can be directly occupied, farmed, or built on. The new residential towers were built as a collaborative venture between the village resident committee and a developer. Through leasing the land-rights-use to the developer the villagers become shareholders in the project and those who lived on the land previously received a preferential price on an apartment. The excess apartments are sold to outsiders or other urban residents from inner Dongguan, with profits being split between the developer and the village co-operative. Currently this model is expedient and highly profitable, explaining the construction of three residential towers in just two years. This wave of residential development synchronizes with China's inflated housing-market bubble, which the government has since been trying to cool down.[25] Throughout these edge-regions of Dongguan, residential housing towers are replacing factories and village houses. In just thirty years, farmland has succumbed to the city both in name and character.

25 Branigan, Tania.
"China Attempts to
Deflate its Unstable
Property Bubble"
The Guardian. 9 March
2011. Accessed
18 June 2012. http://
www.guardian.co.uk/
business/2011/mar/09/
china-deflate-property-
bubble?INTCMP=SRCH

Adaptation: From Looseness to Control

Mr. Liu Zufa: We're performing duties as a government whilst doing business as a company. ... It will change but now that's the situation.

The shequ policy is indicative of the government inventing new regulations to try and bring the system of land transformation back under control. The early period of the 1980s released powerful economic forces at a global economic scale that took root by means of the opportunities that were opened up to rural villages and local entrepreneurs.

These opportunities were facilitated by means of the differences between urban and rural citizens and the ability of rural citizens, and particularly rural village co-operatives, to utilize their land-rights-use as a commodity. As a mechanism to counter this rampant and indeterminate development, the shequ policy relinquishes control away from individuals and their own rights of land use and places it within the control of the village co-operative. For rural villagers this means that they now have to forgo pretty much all of their past livelihood to become shareholders within the collective enterprise. Although it could be argued that villagers have always been part of the collective entity of the village, the evolution of the collective itself has been profound. No longer just being charged with decisions regarding agricultural quotas, as was the case prior to reform, the village co-operative, as in the example of Jian Sha Zhou, is a highly organized business involved in numerous investments and dealings with outside stakeholders, such as property developers and foreign investors. As well as this, the entrepreneurial zeal open to villagers and choices about their own land-use-rights has been stifled. If the earlier period demonstrated the potential for conflicts to emerge as a result of disagreements relating to legal land contracts within a climate of rapidly changing policies, the future period will probably see more conflicts emerge between villagers and the co-operative leadership itself. [26]

26 Guo, 2001

As the shequ policy takes force in areas such as Dongguan it is likely that more grievances will take effect as the co-operative takes on more of the villagers' assets. There is an evident potential contradiction between what is necessarily good for the villagers and what is best for the business of the co-operative. When money is free flowing through the hierarchical strata then all is fine. Yet surely, as in any other economic situations, particularly those as unpredictable as China's, these businesses will have their ups and downs. In the down periods it is not unlikely that disenchantment may rise between villagers and local officials or mistrust over certain dealings between local officials and private developers. There are probably many cases where this is already happening. There are also numerous opportunities for corrupt practices and mechanisms to seek out grey areas of land policy and methods of expropriation. What links all of these issues is the designation and transformative process, both in character and in legality, of rural to urban land. The most vulnerable sites and where contestation appears most apparent are at the periphery of cities. As the city boundary is extended and rural land is subsumed into urban land the discrepancies between different policies become manifested through contestation. The instability of the edge in China is an emerging urban territory that has been shaped by a succession of policies whose future implications are yet unknown.

Tongjiang Village

RECYCLED BRICK SCHOOL

Urbanizing the Rural

↗ A landscape of generic construction and unfinished buildings, Jiangxi, 2010

Tongjiang village in Jiangxi Province southeast China is a village on the verge of change. The village consists of approximately 5,000 farmers growing crops of lotus seed and tobacco with yearly incomes of about 1,700 RMB ($260 US). The village is part of Xiaosong Town, which contains fourteen villages with a total population of 35,093 that in turn is part of Shicheng County having a population of 302,000, with the majority of the population (84.76%) having rural hukou. Driving from the town to the village one can see numerous construction sites as old village structures are replaced by concrete framed houses with brick infill and typically clad in ceramic tiles. Many are unfinished revealing different phases in the building process. Some remain in various states of incompletion—lacking tiles or windows—and in some instances the ground floor is finished and occupied while the upper levels are left until money becomes available for their completion. Along the main road the dominant typology is a version of a shop-house with a ground floor unit used for commercial purposes—often material suppliers, motorbikes, or mobile phone shops—with the floors above cantilevered out to create a protected area below. Other buildings such as schools and dormitory blocks are three-to four-story concrete slab blocks with single-loaded corridors, rendered and painted white.

Arriving at Tongjiang village there were further signs of the urbanization process. Adjacent to the school site, older village houses were being replaced by much larger residential blocks, which we learned were part of a government settlement plan to create new homes for villagers who were being compensated for their land from another site, closer to the town. Further government plans for the area were not made accessible to us, however regulations stipulated that all buildings had to be set back from the road indicating that it is likely that the road will be expanded in the near future.

Working with the charity World Vision, the brief was to expand the existing school from 220 children to 450 through the creation of a new building with eleven classrooms to provide a learning hub for a network of rural villages. The government's intention was to close smaller village schools in more remote rural locations in favor of a larger school closer to the developing urban areas. This consolidation also signified that Tongjiang, rather than the other surrounding villages, had been selected for further development.

↙ Student visions of
their ideal school

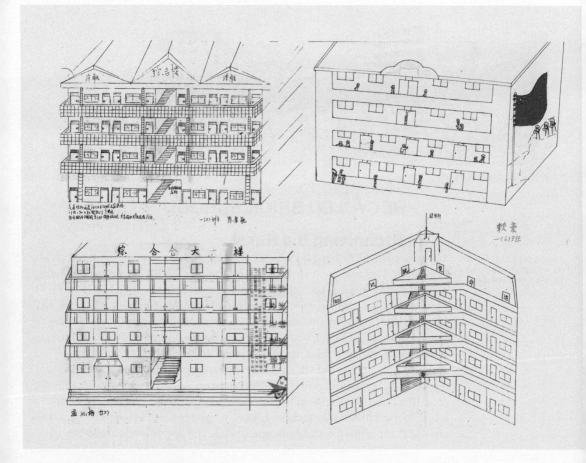

↗ The site before
construction, 2010

World Vision was interested in how we could challenge the design of the typical school building in China without incurring major additional costs. As part of their initial research they organized a workshop with local school children and asked them to draw their ideal school building. Surprisingly, the majority of the students drew buildings that resembled the very same, existing generic type. This demonstrated that these children simply had not witnessed other possibilities for school design and that their imagination for other ideas was limited by knowledge, education, and what they see in their everyday environment. This is not a critique, more a realization that in order to offer any alternative and not be faced with resistance against something alien and unknown, the project had to be convincing in offering practical solutions— better insulation, good natural light and ventilation—and spaces that could be advantageous to both the school and the village. Through many rounds of on-site meetings and dinners with local officials, the head teacher, and the local design institute, who were responsible for administering the building code, the design was accepted. Given the limited constraints in budget, materials, and construction knowledge, the project aimed to produce a building that could create unique spatial experiences for learning and social interaction that in turn could demonstrate that school buildings do not have to all look the same. Our approach was not to return to the vernacular but was driven more by a desire for difference: to offer an alternative to generic building and to prioritize local specificity.

Material Recycling

The site is at a T-junction between a road that is flanked by shop-houses on either side and connects to the town and a small road that leads to the village and lotus fields beyond. On one side of the track leading to the village there are a few mud brick out-house buildings while the back of the site contains rows of newly constructed four-story residential slab blocks. This is the new village: a resettlement community built as compensation for village land being developed elsewhere. This site clearly depicts a fragmented terrain of residual agricultural buildings and new construction. Even the verge between the main road and the edge of our site was being used by locals growing vegetables for their own use.

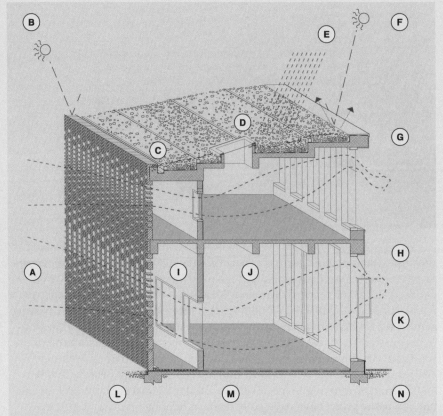

A   Southerly prevailing summer winds: pass through brick screen, cooled by shaded corridor before entering classrooms

B   High summer sun: no sunlight penetration to interior, minimal solar gain to south-facing wall

C   Wide gutter: accommodates heavy rain flow

D   Rooflight: improves daylighting, increases solar gain

E   Rain water (heavy in summer): run-off slowed + partially stored by rubble/plant growth on roof

F   Midsummer sun from north (almost directly overhead): minimal overhang + deep recess provide shading

G   RC roof slab with rubble over: increases thermal mass

H   Top hung windows: shed rain

I   Shaded cooling corridor

J   Classroom

K   Side hung windows: to increase air-flow in summer

L   Perforated brick screen wall, internal face painted white to increase lighting levels through reflectivity

M   Masonry partition with opening windows: for natural lighting + cross-ventilation

N   Glazed screen with brick piers

Strategically the new building is positioned along the road's edge to create an open public space between the new building and the existing school. The building acts as a buffer—a thickened edge—that frames the open space of the playground. The naturally sloped site was terraced into two levels with a height difference of around 2 meters. This topography was manipulated to create a series of outdoor steps that stretch from the main entrance across the building and through to the courtyard beyond. This creates a protected open-air meeting room that is directly accessible from the street which can be used for local village meetings or events. The level change advantageously produces a large assembly hall at ground level that also functions as a community learning space or library. At the entry to the building a stair leads up to the first floor, which stretches across the site's entire edge. Roof-lights puncture this space providing direct light that animates the corridor and classroom spaces throughout the day.

Material from a demolished administrative building was mixed with other waste bricks that we collected from nearby demolition sites. As the urbanization process commences, more and more buildings are erased to make way for larger infrastructure or redevelopment plots. Some of these buildings were constructed from local "blue" or "green" bricks that are predominantly grey in color. Today these bricks are no longer produced, or only produced at a very high cost, and have been replaced by inferior quality bricks that are always hidden behind tiles or concrete render. The intention is to make use of this abandoned material by redeploying it in innovative ways.

The roof is formed from low quality recycled brick fragments and rubble that thickens the roof to provide additional thermal mass. This cools the building in summer and helps the classrooms retain heat during the winter. The rubble acts as a substrate for natural greening from windblown plants, mosses, and lichens. The roof steps down to join the wall, which was intended to gradually become more open through perforations in the brick patterning. This external skin protects the internal classrooms from excessive solar gain yet allows for natural ventilation throughout the teaching spaces. This wall was to be constructed from a mixture of recycled grey and red bricks depending on what we were able to collect. Unfortunately the local design institute did not approve the design, citing structural reasons as new legislation for earthquake resistant structures was brought in after the 2008 Sichuan tragedy. In order to maintain the performance of the wall, we swapped the bricks for concrete

↘ The roof: the brick rubble is a substrate for windblown plants.

→ Entrance and colored painted columns

↓ The outer perforated wall and brick inner facade

blocks, which we turned on their side to allow the wall to maintain its porosity. The leftover bricks were used to make the stepped topography of the seats and the outdoor classroom.

← pp. 114/115: The outdoor
assembly space and
courtyard facade

↓ Playing in the spaces
between the columns

    The initial design was to have a more solid brick facade on the outside with a more transparent interior facade wall made of vertical concrete fins and glazing to the courtyard side. As the exterior wall was now made of concrete blocks, we exchanged the materials to use brick fins on the interior facade. The fins vary in size for different functions: thin strips prevent solar glare and wider C-sections contain bookshelves within the classrooms. The rhythm of the facade oscillates between going from thin to thick and is differentiated between the first and ground floors to create a visually dynamic composition.

Innovation with Limited Resources

Through an emphasis on the potential of waste material, simple environmental strategies, and the creation of a diversity of learning spaces, both indoor and outdoor, the school is robust and adaptable enough to withstand the potential transformation of the surrounding context. The library or meeting room exemplifies this approach. The room is to some extent over-scaled—it is a double-height and around the length of two classrooms. Rather than prioritize a singular function such as a library, art room, or assembly hall we decided to allow the school to determine its program. The space can be easily subdivided and can even accommodate a mezzanine level that connects back to the landing level of the external stair. This way, by providing an infrastructure for possible uses, the school and the village can adapt the space according to their future needs.

    Through innovating within limited resources of budget, craft, and technology in terms of program, material, and environmental strategies, the objective is to create a school that is a prototype for sustainable rural development. It responds to the specific forces of transformation within its context yet stakes a claim to an architecture that is not overly nostalgic or vernacular in nature. New models and approaches must be continually sought to challenge the status quo of generic building construction. It is not simply a question of a future that is rural or urban, rather there need to be mechanisms that allow for the rural to evolve, rather than be completely subsumed by urban territory.

Angdong Village

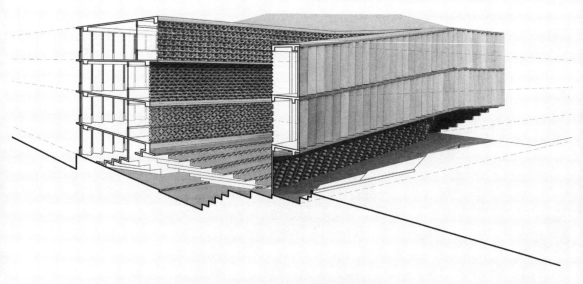

RURAL INSTITUTIONS

The project for Angdong Village is to design a charitable hospital, the first of its kind in China. Rural healthcare in China currently faces a multitude of challenges. Beginning in the 1950s the main healthcare providers were "barefoot doctors" who had only basic training and provided rudimentary procedures. The first organized system of healthcare was established in 1965 with the "Cooperative Medical System." The primary focus was upon illness prevention and health education, with villagers essentially sharing expenses for treatment and medicine. This early period of healthcare was considered very effective when compared to other developing nations at the time. However after the dissolution of the people's commune system in 1980, subsidies for hiring doctors and hospitals also ended. This left the villagers on their own, and by 1990 only 5% of rural villagers had purchased health insurance. In addition

they preferred to be treated in city hospitals and as a result many rural hospitals subsequently failed. Recognizing these problems, in 2002, a new system of rural healthcare was created under the "New Rural Cooperative Health Care Scheme." This scheme primarily provided subsidies and organized top down healthcare insurance for rural areas. However the scheme has led to systematic overcharging and prescription of unnecessary exams and treatments as a means to raise income for doctors and hospitals. Commissioned by the Institute for Integrated Rural Development, a Hong Kong charity, our task was to develop a model rural health care building, capable of supporting the many progressive reforms on rural hospital management and caregiving.

Currently the healthcare building is a three-story rectangular block in the village that was adapted from a school building. An exterior central stair means that patients must be carried up (often on the backs of relatives) to receive treatment. In addition there is no provision for a waiting room. Our design provides some of these basic necessities. As one of the few rural institutions that exist (the other predominant type is the school building) our goal was to define these institutions as public buildings. Therefore our building has an enclosed courtyard space that is wrapped by an accessible ramp from the ground floor to the roof. This creates a vertical public space for in-patients and family members. The ramp is wide and contains spaces for seating, allowing patients to get a breath of fresh air. At the ground level, the courtyard has additional steps for seating and functions as an outdoor waiting area and even a space for village events.

↖ The preliminary site formation around the existing hospital building

↪ p. 122: Variations in the screen block

The sequence of construction is simple and orchestrated to maintain the hospital services during construction. First an L-shape building would be constructed in the remaining site around the existing hospital block. Upon completion, the hospital would relocate, the old block would be demolished, and finally the ramp circulation would be built in its place. This results in a centralized courtyard building. The ground floor would create an open connection from the road to the landscape beyond the new building.

The choice of materials would further distinguish the inner courtyard from the exterior facade of the hospital. The outside facade is made of old grey bricks recycled from the demolition of a nearby factory building. These traditional bricks, no longer used, allow the new hospital to have the quality of an older historical building. On the inside facade, along the spiral circulation passage, a newly manufactured concrete block would be used. From a distance, these blocks have the appearance of a common type, a circular opening in a square form. However they are cast in a flexible latex mold. A series of blocks are produced where the opening gradually projects outward and rotates within the square form. The inside courtyard gains a soft and smoothly changing quality, casting variable shadows in the sunlight during different periods of the day.

These simple ideas are minor in comparison to the issue of healthcare reform in China, or running the first charitable rural hospital. However the hospital as a public institution is a completely new concept in China. There exist relatively few public facilities, and even schools are walled off and managed as contained programs.The task for architecture could be to change the perception of rural institutions, to conceive them as public, open and accessible to all.

↘ **Assembly of the flexible mold**

↓ **Different screen blocks cast in the flexible mold**

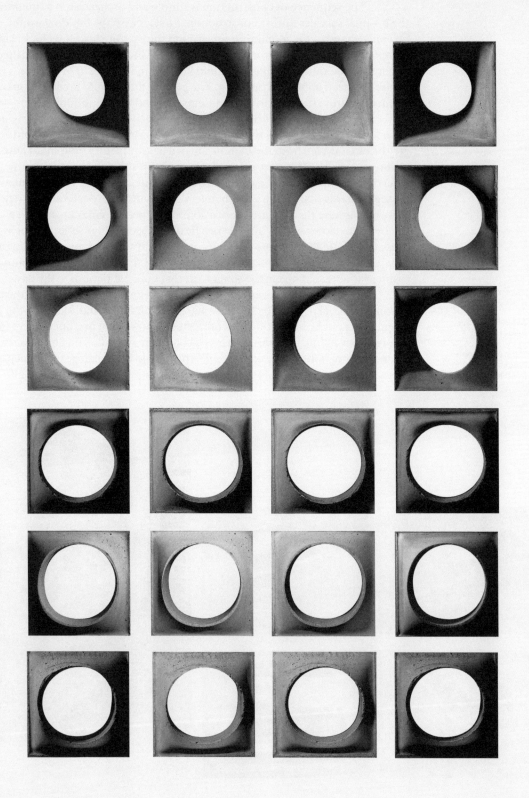

by
Christiane
Lange

Rural Village

THE COUNTRYSIDE IN LIMBO

1   Lefebvre, Henri. 1974.
    *The Production
    of Space.* Blackwell
    Publishers, Oxford

"Every society produces its specific space and spatial code, once in the everyday life and once in the instruments of power." [1]

Throughout the last century, the concept of the "New Modern Socialist Countryside" has made the Chinese rural an ongoing site for experimentation. With consecutive implementations of radical land reforms, in 2013 the countryside has reached a state of limbo: neither modern nor traditional, industrial nor agrarian, new nor old, rural nor urban. What led to this interrupted spatial code? What are its spatial characteristics and how has this spatial condition shaped local culture?

This article investigates these aspects using the case study of Luk Zuk Village. It examines four main phases that have affected the current spatial code of the Chinese rural: Ancient Tradition, Collective Memory, Affiliated Migration, and Consumption and Construction.

Luk Zuk Village

Luk Zuk is a small village in Guangdong Province surrounded by green rice fields, limestone mountains, and rock formations. It is one of around 600,000 administrative villages—the smallest administrative unit—in the People's Republic of China. The village contains nine sub-villages dispersed between ancient patches of rice fields and fishponds. The traditional gateway or Paifang welcomes visitors to Luk Zuk in the form of a modern concrete gate topped with pink tiles.

At first glance, the scenery of Luk Zuk looks like an ancient Chinese landscape painting. However, on second glance the village reveals many sites for new construction. Concrete foundations, piles of red bricks, and half-finished tiled houses grow like mushrooms between yellow loam pig stalls, traditional green brick courtyard houses, and ancient ancestral halls. Some people live in dilapidated courtyard houses without electricity and water, whereas others have built four-story houses decorated with Romanesque arches and Greek style loggias, and are provided with TV and Internet access. Some old houses and ancestral halls are left empty or used for chicken coops and storage while rice paddies are taken over by construction.

Ancient Tradition

Villages in China have been the basic social unit of its society for thousands of years. Formed through a family clan, the village was a farming community. As in other rural societies, landlords owned the land, with peasants carrying out agricultural production. In Luk Zuk, natural villages emerged around the 17th century and were governed by the Long Clan—the first family clan that settled in the area. With the founding of the People's Republic of China in 1949 and the socialist dream for a "New Society," Luk Zuk and the tradition of the Chinese rural was placed into a new context.

↖ Vacant collective housing complex with mined mountain in the back

Collective Memory

"There is a great variety of units to compose a new society, such as kindergartens, bath houses, schools, libraries, banks, farms, factories, shops, theatres, hospitals, gardens, museums, and councils. Put the new school and new society of this kind together, and it is the New Village." [2] (Mao Zedong, 1919)

In the early 20th century Mao Zedong envisioned a communist utopia, in which the village would become the seed and force for the revolution that would turn China into a modern industrial state.

"Obey peoples' opinions, stimulate power." [3]

With the Agrarian Land Reforms introduced by Mao in 1950, landlord Long Zhaoxiang's land was divided among the nine existing clans of the Luk Zuk

4   Slogan of the rural communes—See: Letian, Zhang. 2008. "Building a New Village: Revelations from People's Communes." *Urban China, Work in Progress, A Timezone 8+ Urban China Production*, pp. 14–17

5   The grain tax for one production team in Luk Zuk was 5,000 kg yearly in 1970.

6   *Hukou*—Caste system that separates rural and urban citizens

7   With the open door policy in 1978 launched by Deng Xiaoping economic reforms were introduced in China. China's GDP grew rapidly from 1978 to 2005. Urbanization exploded and urban and industrial development became finally the long-intended success story of the Modern China.

8   *Collective Land Ownership and Individualized Land Use Rights*—In order to increase agriculture production and to gain more diversity in the crops, the new government gave land ownership back to the village collective, removed the grain tax, and opened the market for villagers.

9   *Temporary Migration*—"October 1984, the State Council announced that peasants working in towns be granted the 'self-supplied food grain' hukou,* marking the first opening in the rigid division of city and countryside." See: Fan, C. Cindy. 2010. "Migration, Hukou, and the City." *China Urbanizes: Consequences, Strategies, and Policies.* The World Bank, pp. 65–90

10   Interview with local resident Mr. Tsui, 22 July 2011. Conducted during the Luk Zuk Summer Workshop July 2011.

area. Every clan cultivated its land and paid a grain tax to the state and surplus was traded on the market. Through the reforms, social equality was established and imperialism destroyed. However, in order to achieve Mao's vision for a modern industrial China, these changes were not enough.

"Collectivity first, individuality second." [4]

For the following thirty years, the lands owned by the clans were merged under collective ownership and went into the ownership of the state. The nine family clans got divided into seventeen production teams to form the People's Commune. They got assigned equal sections of the land to cultivate, state cadres collected the grain, and in return, the production teams were assigned an equal quota of food and daily necessities.[5] Some villagers were sent to work in state owned factories and farms, others built infrastructural projects around the country, but the majority stayed in the village under their rural hukou—their citizen status based on their place of birth.[6]

In the 1970s members of one production team moved from their individual family courtyard houses into collective housing: a rectangular courtyard complex that housed twenty-eight families. The standard of living and status of the peasants did not improve in Luk Zuk under Mao's social order of the collective: the collective housing was based on the same standard as traditional housing, and communal living, state rations, and socialist propaganda now defined the everyday lives of the villagers.

Affiliated Migration

The open door policy and the economic reforms introduced by Deng Xiaoping in 1978[7] did not impact Luk Zuk directly in terms of foreign investment or state owned industry. There was no such success story, compared to other villages that suddenly became extremely rich, merely by being close to economically prosperous areas.

After the launch of the Collective Land Ownership and Individualized Land Use Rights,[8] Luk Zuk's villagers changed how they used their land. The Tsui family signed a fifty-year lease for huge parts of the mountain areas with an American company. The firm exchanged the native eucalyptus trees for a pine plantation for a sum that was less than the cost of a car. The Ma family rented out another mountain to a granite mining business that has slowly removed the mountain's peak, which has had a huge environmental impact on the village. For other families, the reclaimed, tiny plots of land have been barely sufficient to sustain them, with few able to sell any surplus in the now open market.

After the affiliated migration rules of the rural hukou loosened in the early 1980s,[9] Luk Zuk villagers increasingly decided to work in factories, restaurants, or construction sites in cities and send money back to the village to support their families. Only the elderly and children remained in the village. Mr. Tsui is from the second generation of the Luk Zuk village migrants. He has worked and lived in cities for twenty years. Today he stays in the village and takes care of his grandchildren, while his children now work at a restaurant in a nearby town. His wife went back to work in a garment factory after he came back three years ago. "After forty nobody wants you to work anymore, you are too old" explained Mr Tsui.[10]

↙ Mr. Tsui, village head in Luk Zuk

↘ Village construction

Consumption and Construction

Water and power supply did not exist until the late 1980s in Luk Zuk.
The county road, the X424, to the nearest town, Qiaotou, was built in 1995
by the Administration Bureau, while the paved village street in Luk Zuk[11]
was built one year later. Since 2000, under the slogan "Build a New Socialist
Countryside,"[12] the government has promoted rural development. With
reference to Mao's envisioned "New Socialist Countryside," the call to "Build
a New Socialist Countryside" has kick-started an unparalleled construction
boom. The money sent back to the village through the rural diaspora meant
that wealth increased in Luk Zuk. This enabled the first generation of migrant
workers to return to the village. Their families moved out of the collective
housing complexes and started building new houses.

11 The paved village
    street was built as
    co-operative investment
    by the government and
    Luk Zuk villagers.

12 The "Ganzhou Model"
    becomes best practice
    for "integrated rural-
    urban development"
    since 2000. Villages
    have been selected and
    blueprints of houses
    have been developed to
    showcase best practice
    for the "New Village."
    See: Looney, Kristen
    E. 2012. "China's
    Building a New Socialist
    Countryside: The
    Ganzhou Model of
    Rural Development."

13 "China to Boost Rural Construction," CCTV9. Accessed July 2012. http://english .cctv.com/program/ chinatoday/20100201/ 100953.shtml

With the release of the Government's No. 1 Document in 2010, Tan Ming, Deputy Secretary General of the China Development Research Foundation, stated that not everyone can afford new houses. However, China has 700 million people living in rural areas alone, with many becoming more affluent and more able to invest in construction.[13] To encourage this domestic spending, the government subsidized new construction materials, promoted best "New Village" schemes and gave out housing blueprints for multistory "New Village Housing." [14]

14 *Build a New Socialist Countryside*—In March 2006, China's National People's Congress officially announced the central government's intention to "Build a New Socialist Countryside," a new policy initiative and approach to rural development.

While the village migrants work and live in the city, the construction of their "New Housing" booms. The old houses are emptying out and building traditions are being replaced by modern construction methods. The tiny agricultural land plots have turned into construction sites. Meanwhile, agricultural productivity has dropped, with the economic dependency on the city and the diaspora, as well as wealth inequalities, rising.

Rural Limbo

15 See: Critchfield, Richard. 1981. *The Villagers: Changed Values, Altered Lives: The Closing of the Urban-Rural Gap.* Anchor Books

The spatial imprint of the planned social society and collectivization is barely traceable in Luk Zuk today. The Great Leap Forward led to famine in the Chinese countryside with an estimated 30 million villagers dying between 1959 and 1961.[15] However, artifacts and propaganda posters from this time are still found today in village houses. Alongside contemporary canto-pop stars,

Mao is still idolized and celebrated as the father of modernization, present in every rural household's living room, leaving a village with a collective memory of socialist slogans and the suppression of its past.

↙ Last family living in the collective housing complex

The villagers' socio-economic standard drastically changed with the economic reforms after 1978. Urbanization resulted in affiliated migration of the rural society. Increased wealth from the diaspora and injected construction by the government has reduced poverty, but led to land fragmentation and land shortages in the village. Agricultural productivity has dropped yet the country's food demand is increasing with the village remaining economically dependent on the city. In this regard, the Chinese rural can be described as being in a state of limbo. The villager, still under the status of the rural hukou, is still tied to the village yet is economically dependent on the city. Elevated to some extent, but tied to the soil, the villager is neither grounded nor free. This leaves the status of the rural and the urban and the idea of the "New Socialist Countryside" as one of the biggest controversies and challenges of modern China.

Qinmo Village

INCREMENTAL VILLAGE DEVELOPMENT

The Qinmo Village project is a long term, strategic project that has involved several different donors and multiple stakeholders over the course of the last six years to gradually enable the village to become more environmentally and economically self-sustainable. In 2006, Green Hope Foundation selected Qinmo Village, a poor and remote village in Guangdong Province, as the site for a new school with an emphasis on environmental education and good practice. As this village had not damaged its agricultural land with chemical fertilizers or pollutants, there was also an opportunity to help the villagers grow organic farming products that could be sold in the Hong Kong market. The project began initially with the construction of a new school building followed by the conversion of the old school building into a community center and demonstration eco-farm. Working with various donors in seven individually funded projects, the overall focus was on education.

↘ The main road in Qinmo Village

A New School

In China, nearly all school projects being donated follow a simple design: a two- or three-story balconied building and basketball court surrounded by a high wall. Our approach was different. The site was a piece of land on the boundary between the village and the fields. Remaining rice terraces crisscrossed the site. Rather than completely flattening the ground, a strategy of cut and filled earth created an S-shaped edge, along which the school could sit. The building was designed to have a green roof above each classroom that could serve as a student garden. The steps leading up to the roof would face the old village while the classrooms would have a view of the farmland.

Villages in China are characteristically dense and lack public gathering spaces. From the beginning, the school was envisioned as a public building, not just a school for children but a public space for the entire village. During holidays and special times of the year, the villagers use the school as a large outdoor theater and a center of village activity. At a later stage, one of the classrooms was transformed into a library donated by a different charity, the Hope Foundation. The design for the library interior continued the theme of a social landscape by constructing a raised floor with cut away island voids that students could informally sit in while reading.

Though the shape of the school broke away from the tradition of simple rectangular volumes, the villagers readily accepted it since it was interpreted to have positive feng shui and blended well with the landscape. However it was much more difficult to persuade the villagers not to clad the building in generic ceramic tile. Unfortunately because of cost, only a cheap cement brick could be used for the infill walls. We counter-proposed to buy paint and have the students and villagers paint the bricks bright fluorescent

↖ View of Qinmo Primary School from the farmland

↗ Library interior; Exterior facade; Classroom interior

→ The school used for festivals and events

colors instead of tiling over the brickwork. It allowed the school to save money as the finished facade of the school looks similar to a tile pattern. However the painting of the bricks involved the collective participation of villagers—a very different connotation than the mass manufactured tile.

↖ Interior courtyard of the community center

Back to the Old School

The creation of the new school left the old school—a traditional courtyard building—vacant and without apparent use. Another charity, Chinese Culture Promotion Society, worked with an agricultural research organization, Kadoorie Farm and Botanic Garden, to come up with a strategy for the old school's adaptation and reuse. The design of the space involved transforming the school into a community center with very different programmatic requirements. The idea was to create a demonstration eco-household and education center for agricultural techniques. The first step was to divide up the open concrete space into areas that could be filled with soil and planted. An ecological cycle is instigated through linking household waste to the feed for pigs and chickens that in turn produce manure for plant beds testing new plant varieties. A greenhouse nurtures seedlings and the kitchen garden grows herbs for daily use. The agricultural program extends to a farm outside of the village, which is experimenting with economically profitable products—a premium chicken and a tea-tree oil—in order to open up additional markets for the villagers.

A   Chinese Culture Promotion Society (CCPS) and Green Hope work together with the University of Hong Kong (HKU) to design the new school.

B   The Local Government Funds 50% of the construction of the new school.

C   The villagers and local government allow CCPS the permission to renovate and use the old school as a community center.

D   CCPS sponsors the village kids to go to school.

E   Village kids attend classes at New Qinmo School.

F   Village kids attend summer camp / winter teaching program organized by CCPS at the old school.

G   Some of the kids sponsored by CCPS will go on to University.

H   Every summer and winter they return to the village to teach younger kids at the old school.

I   After graduating, some may become teachers.

J   They will teach at the New Qinmo School.

K   Help to organize program for the summer camp/winter teaching program at the old school

L   Chinese Culture Promotion Society and the Kadoorie Farm provide agricultural education for the village farmers at the old school.

M   New crops are grown at the old school and tested in field.

N   CCPS sets up a farm to raise high income yielding chickens.

O   Farmers sell their products at the local market.

P   The profit made is invested back into the old school for education or agricultural programs.

EDUCATION LOOP
Qinmo Village

ORGANIZATION   HKU ⇌ Green Hope ⇌ CCPS

LOCAL AGENT   Local Government   Villager Kids ⇌ Teachers

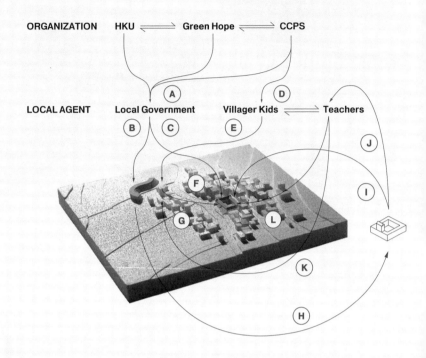

AGRICULTURE LOOP
Qinmo Village

ORGANIZATION   HKU ⇌ CCPS ⇌ Kadoorie Farm

LOCAL AGENT   Villager Farmers

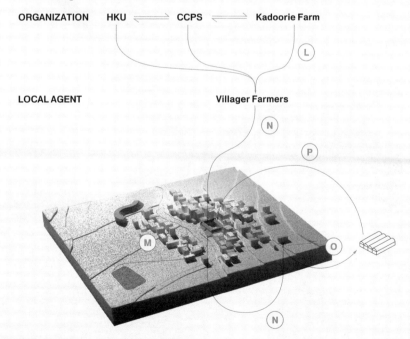

Rural Village   135

We wrapped one half of the courtyard in an L-shape with a concrete screen wall to create additional privacy for the dormitories. In addition, we knocked down a wall to create a covered dining and activity area, which extended into the courtyard. The concrete screen was locally fabricated and consists of two alternate patterns that create a dynamic visual field as one traverses the courtyard. Although these screens are traditionally used singularly for ventilation, we devised a method to construct a 3-meter-high wall by placing them upright and at 90 degrees to each other to create

↑ Screen wall in front
   of dormitories

→ Corridor in front
   of chicken coop

↙ Organic farming
   workshop given
   by Kadoorie Farm

a serrated, self-supporting facade. The ground of the dining room is tiled with a combination of indoor (red) and outdoor (grey) tiles, making a smooth transition between the covered area and the exterior space.

Over time, the old school has grown into an informal community center for the village: village kids spend their lunch breaks reading and playing in the courtyard while the village head uses one room as his office and the open dining area for larger group meetings. Throughout the year the charity organizes several camps for children whom they sponsor to go to school and higher education. These students return to the village and educate the younger children about their experiences. After receiving a scholarship to go to university, each student will in turn be responsible to help sponsor another prospective student. The interaction between the old and new school, through the charity's sustained involvement in the village, has created an educational loop and feedback cycle that encourages children to prolong their learning.

The old school and new school are architectural settings that facilitate social engagement and knowledge exchange. Through promoting sustainable and holistic agricultural practices perhaps the village can incrementally renew an interest in rural productivity while at the same time further the educational possibilities for their children, providing them with alternatives to the mass exodus to the cities. Ultimately this will only begin to rebalance itself if there are economic reasons to stay and, at the moment, the draw of the factory is still too strong.

← Front steps of the community center, providing new seating and planting area

↙ Students pose before practicing the traditional lion dance

↓ Village meeting in the community center

↱ pp. 142–144: Aerial of Qinmo Village showing the community center and the primary school. The photo was taken in 2013, six years after construction.

Luk Zuk Village

RECLAIMING THE ANCESTRAL VILLAGE

Stalemate

↗ The Karst mountain
landscape

Luk Zuk Community Center may never be built. The structural and
construction drawings are complete. The cost estimate is prepared. The
building is ready to go. However, at this critical moment the donation was
withdrawn. Funding can be fickle; priorities can change. Investment by donors
and charities can be complex, with the altruistic goals of the projects and
the economic planning of the organization sometimes pulling in different
directions. It is still unclear why the donor pulled out. Two years ago in 2011
when we visited the site with the donors themselves it was a different story.

Travelling through the Karst mountain landscape to the cluster
of villages within the river valley, the natural beauty of the setting was clearly
apparent. This was new for us as we were more used to working in sullied
landscapes beset by the raw processes of urbanization. Within the village itself

there was a series of other concerns. Visiting teachers, who travelled to this remote location to work at the school, slept in cramped conditions in make-shift beds underneath the staircase. The river was badly polluted, with its banks strewn with rubbish, owing to the villagers' belief that the best way to deal with waste was to throw it in the river where it will be carried away downstream.

    Close to the river was the old village and ancestral hall for the Xu Clan: a traditional walled settlement of courtyard houses constructed from mud bricks, timber, and clay tiles. This complex was mostly seen as an outcast by

↑ The courtyard
and wood stacks

↗ One of the few
remaining residents

↖ The village in its
mountain setting

← Aerial view of old
village

the villagers, disconnected from the main part of the village. The old village was predominantly abandoned—only one or two families remained—and the public space was used for drying timber, stacked up in mound-like structures or collected in bundles. The ancestral hall, despite being neglected, still held symbolic meaning for the villagers even though they had built a new hall in the main village. This was particularly true for the Xu Clan, and the village head, as the elected political leader, became our arbiter for decision making. This was not the first time that we had encountered this phenomenon: throughout rural China traditional buildings have been abandoned in favor of modern alternatives. The idea of the project was to change this mind-set, to bring activities and life back into the old settlement through reconnecting it back to the everyday lives of the villagers. Additionally we addressed the river pollution and provided a place for visiting teachers to sleep.

Prototype

The main stakeholder of the building (but not majority donor) was the Chinese Culture Promotion Society, the client for the old school in Qinmo. The donor wanted to test if the model of the old school could be replicated as a prototype for community use within Luk Zuk. Her charity was already active in sponsoring local children to go to school and so she wanted another site to operate her summer and winter camps. Learning from the old school that the building could be mutually beneficial to local villagers she wanted to provide an event space—open to village use for education, play, meetings, weddings, or whatever they wanted. Through allowing the villagers to participate and use the space, the idea was that they would evolve into becoming more active stakeholders, eventually taking ownership and responsibility for operating and sustaining the building.

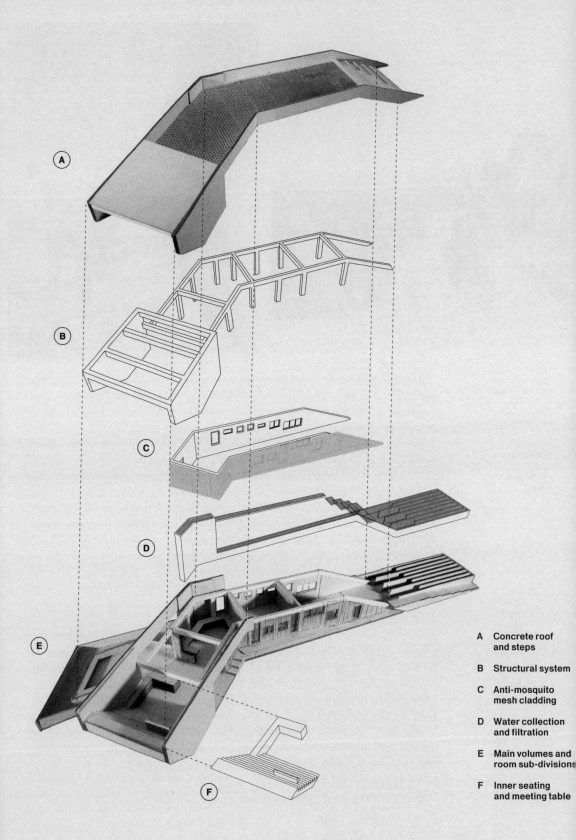

A   Concrete roof
and steps

B   Structural system

C   Anti-mosquito
mesh cladding

D   Water collection
and filtration

E   Main volumes and
room sub-divisions

F   Inner seating
and meeting table

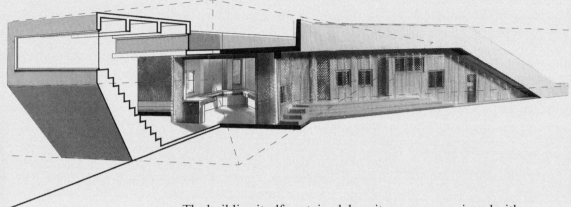

The building itself contained dormitory space, equipped with toilet and shower facilities, for visiting students and teachers undertaking educational workshops. Positioned against the edge wall of the site the private rooms followed this axis while the public event space projected into the existing courtyard to disrupt the overall gridded organization and generate new relationships between the existing ancestral hall and the new building. The building was left as open as possible with only the most private spaces requiring sealed walls, which were further wrapped in a mesh screen to prevent mosquitoes from entering. The continuous roof and ground plane was designed as a machine-landscape, facilitating the collection, reuse, and filtration of water. Water would be collected and harvested from the roof and reused in the kitchen and bathrooms, black water from the toilets would be separated in a septic tank with the grey water entering a series of natural reed-bed channels to filter the water before percolating into the nearby river.

↗ Concept

← Component parts

↓ Site model

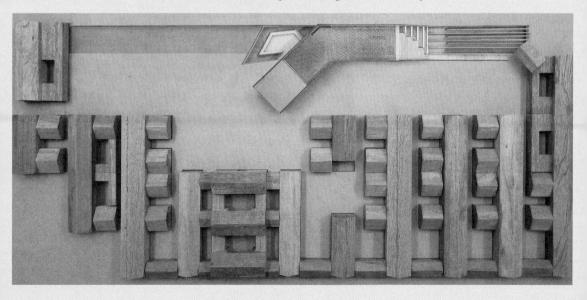

Engagement

Throughout the design process we initiated presentations to the local villagers and village head. However, the model so often presented by architects of an idealized participation between themselves and villagers, simply did not occur. Initially we wanted to convert an abandoned house for the teachers' lodging and we were given approval by the village head. However, as soon as we started the survey we were quickly and adamantly shooed away by the owner, who had no idea about the project. The act of commencing design and visiting and documenting the site was met with skepticism but also a renewed interest from the villagers. They began to see the site that they had ignored and laid to waste in a different light—as an opportunity and as a way to have something for free. The loss of the major financial donor also represented a massive loss of trust on the part of the villagers themselves. As soon as they heard the news, they began to contest the terms of the contract considering it null and void. However, we were told that this opposition to the scheme was mainly from the older residents and that any decision on the future of the site would have to wait until the younger people had returned home from their factory jobs during the official holidays. Asking the donor whether we should try and engage the villagers more in the process, she wisely reflected that the villagers will only realize how much they benefit from the project once it is there and they start to use it. This was proven to be the case in the old school, Qinmo. Whether this will happen in Luk Zuk remains to be seen. Even if the project is not built, it still has got the villagers talking and thinking about a site that they had forgotten and neglected. This void has, at least momentarily, become an active presence in the collective consciousness of the village.

↓ Presentation to village head and villagers

Mulan Village

EDUCATIONAL LANDSCAPE

↗ Huaiji town

Mulan village is located just outside of Huaiji, a town of approximately 100,000 people in Guangdong Province. The journey from Guangzhou to Huaiji used to take over six hours across rough tracks and along mountain contours. Now, a new highway that tunnels directly through the topography cuts the time down to around two hours. As a result Huaiji town is expanding and becoming more urban in character: there are active commercial streets and many construction sites. The peripheral villages however remain distinctly rural in character. Another major infrastructural change is the construction of the high speed rail from Guangzhou to Guilin. The construction of the line involves massive earthworks and the creation of numerous viaducts that bisect farmland and straddle over clusters of village houses. In one village, the size of the foundation of one supportpier is approximately the same as a village house. The project site directly backs onto the construction of the new train line yet is protected by a natural embankment. From this ridge one can view the enormity of the cut through the landscape, exposing the terracotta colored earth as the railway extends linearly in each direction.

Working with the local education bureau and a Hong Kong-based charity, we were asked to expand an existing primary school by adding an additional building containing six classrooms. The motivation behind this expansion was the bureau's desire to consolidate the total number of primary schools in the county. In this process, some older schools will be demolished and others enlarged to make up for the loss. These larger schools will attract children from a larger geographical sphere. The donor of the project, a neurosurgeon, visited the site during the monsoon season and witnessed the flash-flood effect of surface water that poured off the hillside and onto the existing school building, seeping through the walls and into the classrooms. This building is a simple block, with rendered white walls and a tiled roof with an overhanging eave supported on columns. The building forms part of an edge of a wall that frames a simple courtyard. Typically this building would be demolished, however we wanted to retain and integrate it into the composition of the whole site. Below the school, vegetable plots and planting areas gradually slope down to the river. There is a small cluster of houses adjacent to the school; one contained a pile of grey bricks that were stacked outside a mud-brick chicken coop.

Apart from the courtyard of the existing school, the residual external spaces were left bare with an area behind the school scraped of all undergrowth and pushed into a steep, earth slope. The donor was perplexed why this space had been left in an incomplete state and was concerned that the heavy rains might cause this slope to collapse.

↑ The massive earthworks for the high-speed rail

↖ The foundation for the viaduct

The strategy of the design was not only to add buildings but also to organize the site through the creation of a series of inter-linked open spaces. These open spaces would have their own characteristics and uses: small shaded areas, large playgrounds, open classrooms, teaching gardens, and pocket spaces. The first move was to break open the wall of the existing courtyard to connect the old school with the new school building. From there a concrete plane defines the form of the building. Initially rising from the ground as a series of steps to form a new public space and outdoor classroom, the plane becomes the roof before dropping down to form a ground surface that defines the edge of the courtyard. This is infilled with old grey bricks, bought from the local villager next door. The concrete steps, which can be used for school assembly, lectures, or village meetings, are punctuated with small micro-courtyards that light the undercroft below. The library is partially situated

⇢ pp. 154/155: Aerial view of the high-speed rail, old and new schools, farmland and the river

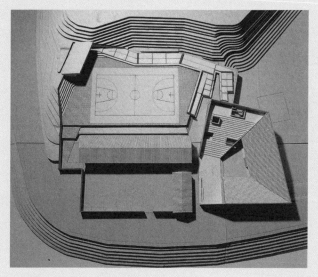

↗ Site strategy

↘ Classroom with framed
 views of landscape
 beyond

under these steps. It has its own courtyard for reading, which also encourages cross-ventilation. The roof is clad in old tiles collected from numerous villages in the local area as old buildings are demolished. At two moments the roof tiles extend down to become vertical walls, which direct water off the roof into ground drains. In contrast to this rough tile, smooth mirror-tiles are deployed on the courtyard facade and on the vertical faces of the steps. This creates visual mirages and distorted reflections that are animated as the children play in the courtyard and on the steps during break time.

The majority of school toilets in China are abysmal and Mulan's was no exception: a small brick hut with dirt pits, no running water, and rank smell. We deployed three strategies: to open both sides of the roof to maintain fresh air; to collect rainwater so that the toilets can be flushed regularly; and to develop a septic tank and reed-bed filtration system to filter the water and remove toxins. The reed-bed is built into the slope at the back of the site,

reinforcing the earth to prevent slippage. The channels bifurcate and split apart to create small discovery gardens and play spaces. As they step down, following the natural contours of the site, concrete seats and steps are inserted for viewing the playground and basketball court.

When this second phase of the project is completed, the constellation of open spaces will create an educational landscape allowing the life of the school to use these "outdoor rooms" during different periods of the day. Our intention is that the school is open to the community so that they can make use of the open forum, library, or any of the outdoor areas. As the urbanization of Huaiji begins to expand and encroach on the village, through the provision of these common, shared areas, the school can become a community focal point and active site for discussions, meetings, study, play, or relaxation.

← pp. 156/157: The school and village

↖ The kids animate the external spaces of the school

Shijia Village

MODERN AND TRADITIONAL HOUSE

Shijia Village is located in the northwestern province of Shaanxi, near the city of Xian. The project examines the idea of the vernacular village house and proposes an alternative, contemporary prototype. Initially it began as a summer workshop with students from the University of Hong Kong. All the houses in the region around Shijia Village are originally of mud brick construction and occupy land parcels of the same configuration: 10×30 m. Within these plots, the villagers are gradually renovating and altering their original courtyard buildings. Traditional elements are fused with new brick and concrete building parts. Often over one-hundred-year-old mud buildings are transformed into animal or storage sheds. Apart from the identically defined plot boundary, no two houses are alike. Students documented and interviewed various families in the village attempting to understand how changes in their economy and social structure resulted in new spatial configurations for the house. Collectively this acts as a portrait of the modern Chinese village house: a portrait not only of building types but of a lifestyle in transition.

↘ All house plots
are 10 × 30 m.

Although the houses have changed in appearance, the courtyard remains an important component of the home. Often the courtyard is simply a leftover space in between older and newer structures. In addition, the courtyard now has to accommodate small vehicles and more modern farm equipment. However in the Chinese context, rural livelihood is still best expressed through the utilization of the domestic courtyard. Traditionally, the courtyard has many formal functions. Given the dense arrangement of house plots, the majority of a village's open space is contained within the walls of the house. This sets up an intimate relationship between the courtyard and other interior rooms that is both visual and functional. Our house design includes four functional courtyards as the primary elements of the house. The courtyards are inserted throughout the house to relate to the main functional rooms: kitchen, bathroom, living room, bedrooms. In addition each courtyard is spatially unique. The design prioritizes the programmatic integration of the courtyards and asserts that the courtyard is the fundamental component of the rural house.

The modern rural house has had to adapt to changes in materials and building methods. Perhaps the biggest change to rural housing is the reliance on outside contractors. Because most able-bodied villagers have left to work in cities, the hiring of outside labor and materials has replaced collective self-construction. Instead of house building as an activity that would bond villagers together, it has become an expression of individuality. The physical transformation of the village is simply a symptom of a larger shift from economic self-reliance into a system of dependency, threatening the very concept of a rural livelihood.

↑ Houses are undergoing transformation from traditional to newer constructions

↗ Drawing of a village house

→ Portrait of a rural family

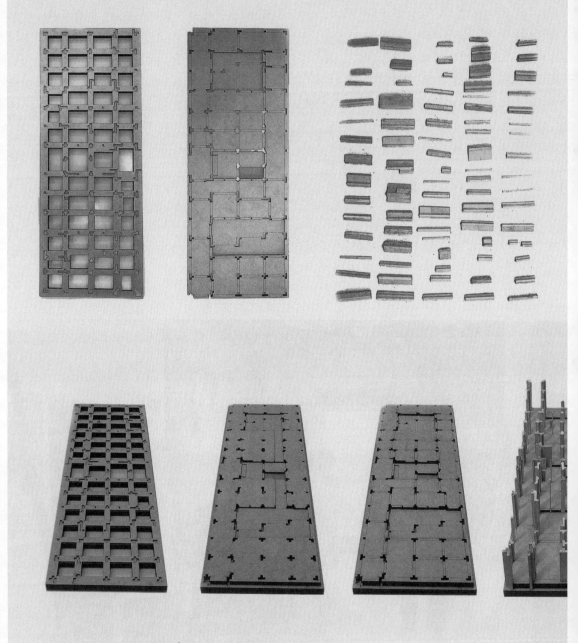

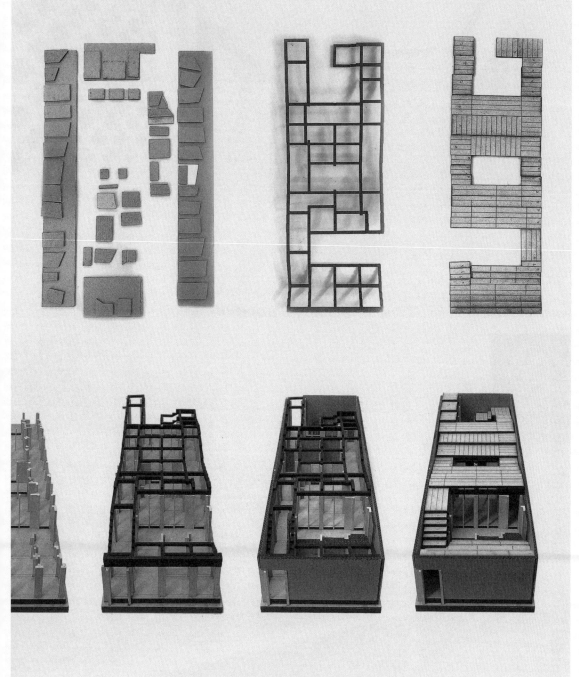

← pp. 162/163: Model of the house design, demonstrating the sequence of construction

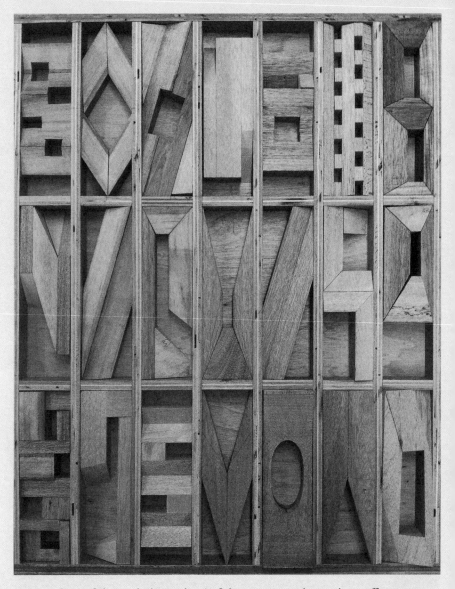

↗ Design exploration of different courtyard arrangements

↖ Courtyard with underground biogas tanks and adjacent animal sheds

← Courtyard with access to the roof

↪ pp. 166/167: Aerial photograph

One of the main intentions of the prototype house is to offer an alternative to the villagers' increasing dependency on outside goods and services to become an example of self-reliance. The roof is multifunctional, providing a space for drying food, steps for seating, and, in the rainy season, a means to collect and store rainwater so that it can be used during the long and dry summers. The courtyards house pigs and an underground biogas system that produces energy for cooking. Smoke from the stove is channeled through the traditional *kang* or heated bed before it exits through the chimney.

The structure of the house brings together old and new. A concrete column and roof structure is combined with mud-brick-infill-walls, mud brick being a traditional means of insulation. Unlike the traditional mud structure, the new hybrid satisfies the criteria for earthquake resistance. The brick is used as a partial formwork to pour the concrete columns. The entire outside wall

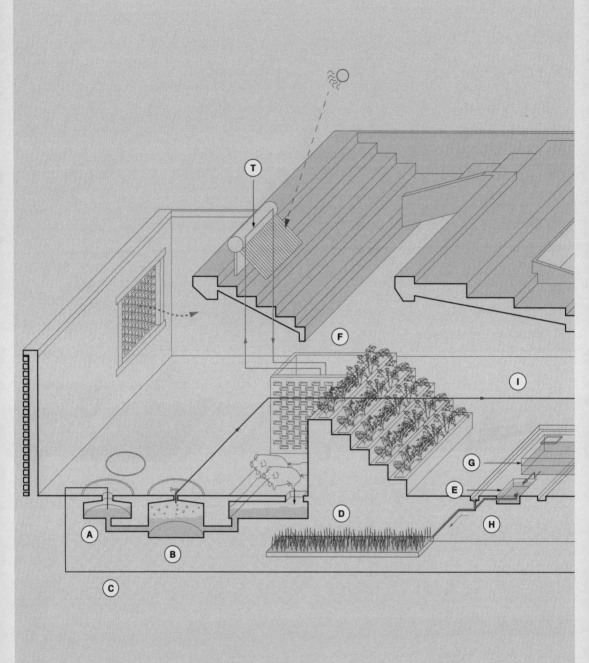

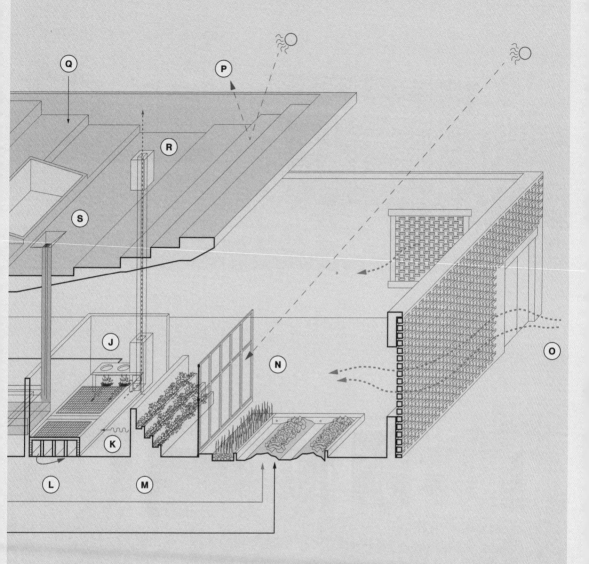

A Slurry	**H** Grey water flows to reed bed / Filtered water for irrigation	**M** Trombe wall heated through greenhouse glass; rammed earth construction acts as thermal mass	**Q** Roof used to collect rain water
B Biogas pool			**R** Chimney
C Dug out and used as fertilizer	**I** Biogas for cooking		**S** Water filter
D Reed bed system for water filtration	**J** Kitchen	**N** Winter sun directly shines on greenhouse glazing	**T** Solar water heater
E Water for washing and cooking	**K** Heat Radiation from Trombe wall	**O** Summer breeze passes through brick screen	
F Toilet	**L** Smoke passes underneath the bed to provide heating	**P** Summer sun is shaded by roof	
G Water storage			

of the house is wrapped in a brick screen, an idea common to vernacular houses in Xinjiang Province in western China. This not only serves to protect the mud walls, but also shades windows and openings. By combining vernacular ideas from other regions of China as well as existing and new technologies, the design is a prototype with both modern and traditional attributes.

Working with the Luke Him Sau Charitable Foundation and the Shaanxi Women's Federation, the program of the house continues to help assert village independence. It will be both a home for women as well as a new center for

← View of house
  facade

→ Construction of biogas
  tank in the courtyard

↘ Mud bricks for the
  walls of the house

women's handicraft. In this manner it is both domestic and communal, a bridge between the individual and collective identity of the village. The construction of the house initiated a new phase for the village economy, developing a new cooperative business around traditional straw weaving. The products are modern designs made in a traditional manner. Rather than accepting the influence of cities, the house project works against this trend, helping to find independent economic strategies for the village.

↖ Straw weaving
in the house.

The house design is a reaction against the prevalence of generic multi-story concrete, brick, and tiled village houses. These constructions are taking place in every village in China. They look the same whether they are located in the far north or in the south. Generic buildings are replacing very specific vernacular house types, which have adapted gradually over hundreds of years to the climate and location where they exist. The design offers suggestions and ideas for combining existing technologies. Certain small improvements have been made for the use of biogas or even rainwater collection. Most importantly, it is an advocate for adaptation as opposed to abandonment of traditional modes of living. Currently, the process of rural development increasingly favors the new. However with only two types of rural housing available, the traditional mud house or a brick and concrete house, the design attempts to bridge between the two. By demonstrating a third option utilizing concrete, brick, and mud, we hope to help preserve the intelligence of local materials and techniques. As a result of the investigation into the modern village vernacular, the project was conceived to represent an architectural attempt to consciously evolve vernacular house construction in China.

Jintai Village

TABULA RASA VILLAGE

Jintai Village is located near Guangyuan, Sichuan, one of the places that was hardest hit by the May 12 Wenchuan Earthquake of 2008. The disaster left nearly 5 million people homeless. It is estimated that 80% of all buildings in the affected area were destroyed. Over the past five years a major reconstruction effort has ensued. However in July 2011, after heavy rainfall and landslides in the region around Jintai Village, many of the newly rebuilt homes and some still under construction, were once again destroyed. This left villagers without further donations or support from the government.

Reconstruction

Since September 2012, we have been involved in a second reconstruction effort for twenty-two families in Jintai Village. This project comes at a time in which many of the affected villages from the Wenchuan Earthquake have been completed. Therefore this project has the potential to serve as a reflection on the initial reconstruction effort as well as to demonstrate a new village prototype and alternative model for redevelopment

Reconstruction can be taken as an opportunity to improve upon the existing state of buildings. Unfortunately the majority of new buildings suffered from corruption, the speed and quality of construction, and a rubber-stamp design strategy. After the earthquake, an entirely new style of building was created. This was typically a simple building of brick and concrete painted on the sides with a pattern that mimicked the wood structure of the traditional mud buildings. The roof was also an imitation of the traditional ceramic tiled roof. Even though from the outside, the buildings seemed to copy traditional ones, the organization on the inside was generic: spaces in these new houses do not vary in scale, are generally larger than necessary, and resemble standardized classrooms rather than responding to specific domestic requirements.

With this observation in mind, our approach to village reconstruction was less concerned with preserving the outlook of the old than with trying to create a contemporary Chinese village. This notion of a contemporary village includes reorganizing the program at the village level and considering

the village as a totality. Not only houses, but community programs, tourism, and the overall farming strategy were incorporated into the design. Although presently, there is a shift away from communal living (villagers no longer live in compounds), by taking the village as a programmatic whole, the economic viability of the village can be strengthened.

↑ Model showing the structure of three different house types

↘ Cast concrete models of houses

Village Ecology

Though the Central Government has invested heavily in rural reconstruction in recent years (not only in the earthquake-affected areas but throughout China) this scheme typically funds only rudimentary facilities and is focused on providing subsidies to individual families for house construction. Our design proposes investment in public programs: reed bed waste-water treatment, rainwater collection, collective animal rearing, biogas facilities, and a community center. The idea is to relate the various programs of the village into an ecological cycle. This is done by linking the spatial organization of the village to its work cycle, by incorporating the village into the landscape, and by creating an environmentally responsive cycle of waste disposal and water usage. By articulating these processes clearly, the village also hopes to become a destination for tourism from nearby urban areas.

The design of the house reinforces interdependency within the village whole. Unlike the house design for Shijia Village (a single story, multiple courtyard house), these houses have several levels and must be arranged in a dense cluster. One challenge was to translate the typical courtyard typology into

← pp. 174/175: Site formation of Jintai Village

a multi-story building. The vertical courtyard functions to bring light and ventilation into the house and to channel rainwater to a storage unit. The courtyard opens up to a public space on the ground floor. Adjacent houses are visually and spatially connected across these spaces. Despite the narrow 3-meter gaps between houses, the ground level of the village remains open and shared.

The design strategy provides four different types of village houses. These are indicated by different stepped roof sections. Collectively they create a landscape that blends in with the mountains beyond. In this relatively dense village, a productive landscape occurs on these rooftops. As space within the village becomes limited, the roof functions as a space for drying food and for additional planting. The infill walls are combinations of various materials, in brick, stone, or mud depending on the program. The aesthetic quality of the village derives from the materiality of its surrounding landscape, allowing it (as in the most traditional of villages) to blend into and become an integral part of its environment.

The notion of a completely new-built village is perhaps stranger than the notion of a tabula rasa city. The village is an ingrained part of Chinese cultural understanding as a place that one originates from. Therefore, the village always seems to have been in existence. With tens of thousands of newly planned villages occurring in China today, the challenge is to reassert the village as an ontological ideal—to plan villages as authentic places whereby the spatial organization and physical expression is derived directly from the relationship to its natural environment. This means conceiving it very differently from the concept of the city.

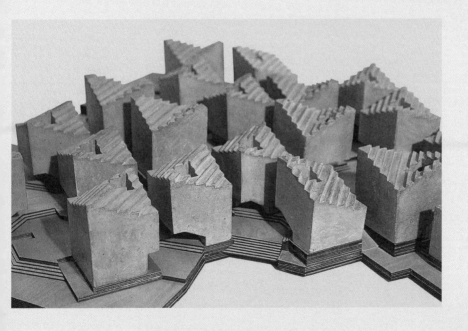

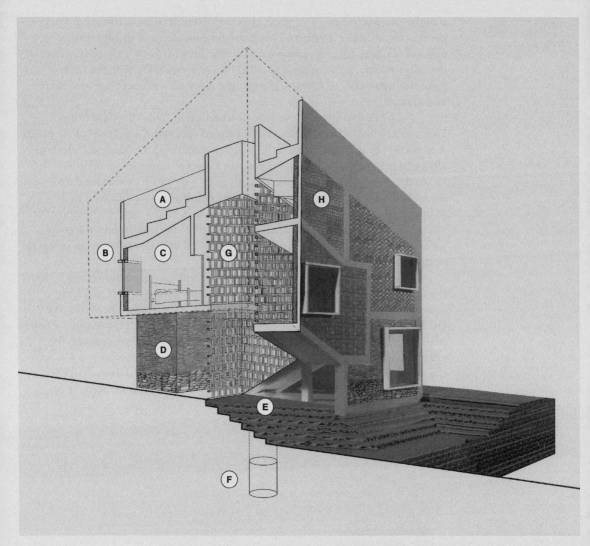

A The green roof is used as an additional recreational and storage area. With options to be used for drying crops, socializing, and planting.

B The exterior walls are a composite of brick with a layer of compressed straw and plaster on the inside. Straw is an excellent thermal conductor, keeping the building warm or cool throughout the year.

C Bedroom

D Entrance

E Courtyard

F Rainwater is collected by the roof and stored in an underground tank.

G The screen wall extends up from the courtyard to the roof, allowing light to flood into the house while aiding cooling and ventilation in the summer.

H The facade is composed of different types of brick infill in the concrete frame structure. Each section has a different pattern, texture, or structure, according to the needs of the interior program.

Changliu Village

FAILING TO PLAN A CHINESE VILLAGE

↗ Aerial plan view
of one sub-village
in Changliu

Changliu Village is located in Guangdong Province in southern China where entire villages of mud houses are systematically being torn down and rebuilt in concrete and brick. This article describes our participation in a village rebuilding process. We experienced inherent difficulties with that process and eventually failed. The Changliu reconstruction is not just one village but actually three different sub-village projects that were never realized. The reasons have more to do with politics than design, together with an inability to adopt a consensus toward "the common good." This may not be surprising given the gradual de-collectivization of farming since the Mao era.

← Interior courtyards

↓ Washing, tooth brushing, and other activities along the passages of the village

→ One of the sub-villages before demolition

↘ The same view after the houses are torn down

Collective Village

Currently, villages in China allocate individually owned land for farming as well as maintaining other collectively owned plots. Land for building houses is sub-divided from a limited common area that typically surrounds the ancestral home. Newly married male heirs, entitled to their own plot of land and their own house, add their structures to the agglomeration. This results in a fabric that is composed of organized and gridded family based compounds together with a loose organization of other houses that surrounds them. It is a highly dense cluster of buildings where every family member has descended from a single ancestor. Because this land is limited, over time, the immediate family may be separated into several smaller plots of 20–40 m^2 each, embedded within the overall village fabric.

The original single-story mud brick constructions were deemed unsafe and unsanitary, prompting a vast reconstruction effort. Another reason—justified under the guise of the safety regulations—is the government ambition to make villages look more modern. Modernity in China is often interpreted as a desire for a stringent uniformity. Although villagers have been modernizing and rebuilding their homes since the economic reforms of the late 1970s and 1980s took effect, the process has now been formalized by the government. This has resulted in a shift in focus away from individual houses to entire villages. More important than a modern outlook is the underlying government concern to preserve the semblance of conformity, counteracting the increasing display of the disparity of wealth in rural areas.

In general, the government provides a portion of funding (typically up to 20% of the total cost) to each household for the reconstruction, with the remainder contributed by the family. The government also makes provision for basic infrastructure and services. The design of the reconstruction is left to the villagers with only general guidelines required by the government including uniform heights of floors and tiling used. These rules clearly emphasize the consistency in the outlook of facades more than actual planning requirements.

In Shuiweidong Village, the objective is to rebuild 110 village houses based on a gridded plan proposed by the villagers in which each family is allocated a 70 m² plot. The idea is to build foundations suitable for a four-story house so that closely related families, now separated into small individual homes, can be collected together under one roof. Government funding provides each family with enough money to build up to the first story with the

↙ Traditional houses are torn down in favor of new houses.

possibility for further upward expansion. About one quarter of the families currently intend to build a second or third story. The rest save money until they are able to undertake construction. Because of the communal nature of the village planning process (all decisions must be taken together), plot sizes are maximized with only a bare minimum of interstitial circulation space. In many places, only a 1- or 2- meter gap will separate future four-story buildings: the horizontal growth of the village will be replaced by vertical expansion.

Generic Village

Rural villagers have arrived at a solution that mimics the urban villages embedded in large Chinese cities. These urban villages are also characterized by an unregulated density. It is common to have 1-meter-wide slits between buildings allowing little light to penetrate to the ground. Currently, city governments are attempting to resolve these conditions and effectively re-integrate the urban villages into the rest of the city. However, in the countryside, villages are now appearing more like their urban counterparts with similar building types and styles copied and built in place of traditional single-story courtyard houses.

↗ House construction can take many years to complete.

The spread of this generic vernacular follows the path of money sent home by migrant workers. Having spent their time toiling to build skyscrapers and parks while living in dense unsanitary conditions in urban villages, their money is used to build a similar looking condition back home. Even as more people leave villages, the money sent home is deposited into a continuous process of building. Without the possibility of banking investment, villagers prefer to put their money directly into the expansion of their homes, sometimes spending between ten to twenty years to finish a four-story building. In the interim, they often live in half-finished structures with the presumption that future generations will continue to live there. Despite the increasingly migratory status of the rural population, resulting in many villages appearing half-abandoned, there remains a strong cultural tie to these ancestral villages. The majority of migrants still presume that they will return to the village to live after they have made their money working in the city. Despite this, the current status is that villages become increasingly denser with fewer and fewer inhabitants.

Political Village

Our challenge in working with Shuiweidong Village was to persuade the villagers to find a balance between their individual and collective needs. With no one to coordinate village planning, residents immediately put their own space needs ahead of the common interest. When we entered the design process, the reconstruction effort was just beginning. We were initially told that the plan was to incrementally tear down ten houses and rebuild ten. Shelters were erected for the temporarily displaced. Surprisingly on our first visit, we found the entire village demolished; all that remained was an empty construction site surrounded by a squatter settlement with neatly organized piles of individually owned materials and furniture. Sadly, the villagers could not agree that some would have their houses built first while others waited. It was all or nothing and it was eventually agreed that everyone should "suffer" together.

The proposal for Shuiweidong Village consisted of simple zoning and setback requirements. This was combined with the design of new building types that would translate the setback rule into a series of courtyard/balcony spaces for each floor. The design was organized as a series of stacked, changeable floor plans in which the balconies could face in various directions. This addressed the issue that as families expand, different male heirs and their immediate families would reside on separate floors. Although a zoning strategy is a basic component of any urban plan, the self-led political processes typical

↖ Furniture and belongings are piled up during village reconstruction. Temporary shelters stand on the periphery.

in rural areas, and the lack of governmental oversight, results in a high level of density and congestion. Indeed, in Shuiweidong Village, it was seemingly impossible to convince all 110 village families to limit their building envelopes with setbacks. Although the new two- or three-story houses will increase by far the amount of space they currently have, the villagers are unwilling to concede even a small amount for the common good—for public space, ventilation and day-lighting.

Whereas the concern for the quality of common space is thwarted by a stubborn self-interest, the design of the houses is collective and self-similar with very little individual input or variation. Duplicate houses are arranged in rows, with balconies and windows facing the backs of the adjacent row. This is due in part both to the non-hierarchical village planning process (everyone should have exactly the same plot of land) as well as government interest in maintaining an image of order and consistency. As a rule, the villagers must agree upon the same tiling and house type for the entire village. Our design strategy to offer four types of houses to maximize open views and a variety of optional living configurations met with difficulty as it did not comply with government regulations. Perhaps the government is attempting to counter the current image of many villages in which singular multi-story houses dominate one-story mud dwellings: signposts for the increasingly diverse fortunes of village inhabitants. What was once a fairly homogeneous society has, even in villages, become an unequal one in which varying degrees of wealth are expressed through ostentatious Westernized features: it is common to see ceramic details of cornices, lintels, balustrades, and pilasters.

Working between the government and the individual villagers, the complexity of the scenario becomes evident. On the one hand, villagers are eager to cut their ties to the past in favor of modern looking building styles, in the process breaking out of the mold of communal living. On the other, the government struggles to maintain an image of collective growth and harmony.

↘ The process of engagement with villagers: the model shows possible house designs to choose from.

Currently, villages in China no longer resemble an idyllic image of farm life. Instead, they are a collision of urban forms against a rural backdrop, with three types of conditions now prevalent. The first is the traditional village, which appears consistent in style and material, but reflects the disorderly and informal process of slow growth over time. The second, or transitional village, appears as a collage of distinct elements, a backdrop of tiled traditional rooftops punctuated by tall singular buildings of concrete and brick, tiled in brightly colored facades. The third condition, the newly built village, is uniform and consistent, the most homogeneous of all, arranged in strict rows, brand new but empty. In this field, the architect must decide to intervene on the side of villagers to cater to their individual requirements or the government to create a coherent result in order to find a balance between individual and collective ambition.

↖ A newly constructed village

by
David
Grahame
Shane

Future Village

VILLAGES IN THE URBAN FUTURE

The village has acted as a heavily loaded symbolic intermediary in debates about the city for many centuries. With the emergence of the Industrial Revolution, the village became the emblem for a lost community and life of an imagined rural simplicity and authenticity. After the collapse of the old imperial, colonial regimes, architects, planners, and urban designers have become aware of villages as a fundamental, worldwide phenomenon.

Villages are deeply rooted in the human psyche and even though the majority of the world's population is declared urban by the United Nations, what is urban in great swaths of the world includes villages of various types. The ancient imperial village, the industrial village, the desakota village, the favela village, and the informational, meta-village form distinct village types that are all present in contemporary societies around the world. Each of these five types has its own peculiar characteristics and dynamism, interacting with each other within the larger global urban order. With so many variables in each system, and the interactions between people in each system, there is obviously no one single, simple future for the rural, urban, or rur-ban village in the near or far future. Designers have to be aware of many different strategies and have to choose carefully how to intervene as there are ethical and environmental questions that have to be faced. Many villages will probably flood and need to move or adapt, others will run out of water, still others may be abandoned. How to work in these situations has ethical dimensions, as does the choice of materials and consultative processes involved. Villages as the smallest rung of the traditional urban ladder are a place of experimentation and opportunity, where new organizational models and techniques can be tested.

The work of Joshua Bolchover and John Lin in this book contains a catalogue of village conditions, urban, factory, suburban, contested, rural, and closely related to the global urban history outlined here, from imperial to colonial, industrial to post-industrial, from metropolis to meta-city. The young architects have tailored and scaled their interventions precisely to each situation providing a beautiful and exemplary response to each village condition, deeply grounded in their local knowledge of place and community. The book can be read as a local journey, like an ancient scroll painting moving across the page, but it also points to deeper truth that we must be alert to all the conditions that are simultaneously present in our complex and contradictory contemporary global cities.

↳ pp. 188 / 189: Jianhe New Town in Guizhou Province. The town is built for 150,000 villagers displaced by the construction of a nearby hydroelectric dam.

CREDITS

Rural Urban Framework is the collaboration between Joshua Bolchover and John Lin. We are grateful for the support structure provided by the Department of Architecture at the University of Hong Kong. We would like to thank all students who have assisted in projects, attended workshops, or have contributed to research electives. Additionally we would like to thank the core team at RUF who have been extremely dedicated to working in difficult conditions in rural China. Furthermore, we would like to thank Jessica Pyman and Camilla Holmgren for their critical input throughout the production of the book.

All project designs, texts, and images are copyright of Joshua Bolchover and John Lin, Rural Urban Framework (RUF), unless otherwise indicated.

Publication

Editors: Joshua Bolchover, John Lin; Graphic design: Kay Bachmann (B/P); Colour correction: Humme.com; RUF team: Ashley Hinchcliffe, Crystal Kwan, Lam Ka Man, Dylan Mundy-Clowry, Tsang Yin To, Yeung York Tsing

Rural Urban Framework

Rural Urban Ecology exhibited at the Venice Biennale 2010, Hong Kong Pavilion / Team: Thomas Chan, Christiane Lange (Leader), Hui Kin Fung, Mok Chit Yan, Qiu Jiayu; Rural Urban Ecology Map exhibited at the Chengdu Biennale 2012 / Team: Huang Zhiyun

Urban Village

Text: Joshua Bolchover and Mary Ann O'Donnell; Image credits: "Handshake Alley" by Esther Lorenz, "Interviews with migrant workers" and "Ms. Chi, landlady of Mao era dormitory houses" by Elton Lam. Drawing credits: students from Inter Cities, an elective class at the University of Hong Kong: Chan Jo Yen, Huang Yanbing, Lam Ho Yin, Li Siqian.

Yongxin Village

Text: John Lin; Commissioning donor: Yanai Foundation; Design: Joshua Bolchover and John Lin Project team: Chen Beining, Ho King Hei, Maggie Hua, Christiane Lange, Jessica Lumley, Mariane Quadros de Souza, Anna Wan; Project details: May 2010–Sep 2012 / 24,000 m² / 24,000,000 RMB (3,000,000 USD) / 1,000 RMB/m² (125 USD/m²)

Factory Village

Text: Joshua Bolchover; Research team: Liang Zhiyong, Wang Tian Meng; Some of the content of this article was based on a paper titled "Closing the World's Factory: The future of the Pearl River Delta during global recession" given at Architecture in the Age of Empire: 11 Internationales Bauhaus Kolloquium 1–5 April 2009.

Lingzidi Village

Text: John Lin; Commissioning donor: World Vision; Project collaborator: Winview Building Materials & Services Co., Ltd.; Design: Joshua Bolchover and John Lin; Project team: Maggie Ma (Leader), Jeffrey Huang, Huang Zhiyun, Mark Kingsley, Crystal Kwan; Project details: June 2011–September 2012 / Size: 65 m² / 170,000 RMB (27,000 USD) / 2,600 RMB/ m² (400 USD/m²)

Taiping Village

Text: John Lin; Commissioning donor: Wu Zhi Qiao Foundation; Project collaborators: Chongqing University; Engineering advisor: Dr. Xing Shijian; Design: John Lin and students from the University of Hong Kong; Project team: Cheng Hiu Tung, Cheung Wai Nga, Chu Ling Tung, Jiaxin Chum, Gu Lik Hang, Charles Lai, Lau Hiu Yeung, Li Bin, Abdul Yeung, Zhang Xudong; Project details: Sep 2007– Aug 2009 / 200 m² / 200,000 RMB (25,000 USD) / 1,000 RMB/m² (125 USD/m²)

Suburban Village

Text: Joshua Bolchover; Research team: Cheung Lai

Ying, Liang Zhiyong, Dylan Mundy-Clowry; Image credits: "Vacant retail space" by Cheung Lai Ying, "Amazing World," "Teletubby Land," "Entire sections of the mall are empty" by Chan Yat Ning

Yanzhou Village

Text: John Lin; Client: Zhaoqing Development Company; Design: Joshua Bolchover and John Lin; Project team: Liang Zhiyong, Martha Tsang; Project details: 2008–2009 / 33,000 m² / 34,400,000 RMB (4,600,000 USD) / 1,120 RMB/m² (140 USD/m²)

Contested Village

Text: Joshua Bolchover; Research team: Timo Heinonen, Liang Zhiyong, Tian Xuezhu; Image credits: "Patchwork urbanism: the example of Dongguan" © 2011 Google and © DigitalGlobe 2012; The research has been partially funded by the Seed Funding Programme for Basic Research at the University of Hong Kong. This essay is a modified version of "Contested Territory: The evolving spatial geographies of Jianshazhou" undergoing review in the forthcoming issue: Volume 20, *Critical Planning*.

Tongjiang Village

Text: Joshua Bolchover; Commissioning donor: World Vision; Additional donors: Luke Him Sau

Charitable Trust; Design: Joshua Bolchover and John Lin; Project team: Ho King Hei, Crystal Kwan, Christiane Lange, Jessica Lumley, Maggie Ma, Mariane Quadros de Souza, Anna Wan; Project Details: October 2009–April 2012 / 1,000m² / 1,280,000 RMB (170,000 USD) / 1,280 RMB/m² (170 USD/m²)

Angdong Village

Text: John Lin; Commissioning donor: The Institute for Integrated Rural Development; Design: Joshua Bolchover and John Lin; Project team: Maggie Ma (Leader), Jeffrey Huang, Huang Zhiyun, Mark Kingsley, Crystal Kwan, Tiffany Leung, Yau Ching Kit; Project details: May 2011–ongoing / 1,450 m² / 1,700,000 RMB (272,000 USD) / 1,170 RMB/m² (190 USD/m²); Background on the history of rural healthcare in China was provided by the Institute for Integrated Rural Development

Rural Village

Text: Christiane Lange Images: Tsui Ho Cheung.

Qinmo Village

Commissioning donor: Matthew Cheng and Peggy Young, Green Hope Foundation (Qinmo Primary School), Lucy Tsai, Chinese Culture Promotion Society (Qinmo Community Center); Additional donors: Luke Him Sau Charitable Trust,

Hope Education Foundation, Kadoorie Farm and Botanical Garden; Project collaborators: Kadoorie Farm and Botanical Garden, Sacred Heart Canossian College; Design: John Lin (Qinmo Primary School), Joshua Bolchover and John Lin (Qinmo Community Center); Project team: Gary Chan, Tammy Chow, Kenneth Lau, Hugo Ma, Tim Mao, Danny Tang, Abdul Yeung and students from Sacred Heart Canossian College; Project details for Qinmo Primary School: Oct 2006–Sep 2008 / 1,200 m² / 1,200,000 RMB (150,000 USD) / 1,000 RMB/m² (125 USD/m²); Project details for Qinmo Community Center: Sep 2008–May 2009 / 450 m² / 180,000 RMB (22,500 USD) / 400 RMB/m² (50 USD/m²)

Luk Zuk Village

Text: Joshua Bolchover; Commissioning donor: Lucy Tsai, Chinese Culture Promotion Society. Additional donors: Luke Him Sau Charitable Trust; Design: Joshua Bolchover; Project team: Maggie Ma (Leader), Nicholas Ho, Yau Ching Kit Project details: March 2011–ongoing / 485m² / 600,000 RMB (98,000 USD) / 1,200 RMB/m² (200 USD/ m²)

Mulan Village

Text: Joshua Bolchover; Commissioning donor: Power of Love Ltd.; Additional donors: Luke Him Sau Charitable Trust; Design: Joshua Bolchover and John Lin; Landscape design: Dorothy Tang; Project team: Maggie Ma (Leader), Ho King Hei, Huang Zhiyun, Crystal Kwan, Jessica Lumley, Yau Ching Kit; Project details: May 2010– Sep 2012 / 500 m² / 573,000 RMB (90,000 USD) / 1,150 RMB/ m² (180 USD/m²)

Shijia Village

Text: John Lin; Commissioning donor: Luke Him Sau Charitable Trust; Project collaborators: Shaanxi Province Women's Federation, Shaanxi Volunteers Association of Red Phoenix Project, Linwei District Women's Federation, Qiaonan Town Government, Shijia Village Committee; Design: John Lin; Project team: Crystal Kwan (Leader), Huang Zhiyun, Katja Lam, Li Bin, Maggie Ma, Qian Kun, Jane Zhang; Project details: April 2009–March 2012 / 380m² / 325,000 RMB (53,400 USD) / 855 RMB/m² (140 USD/ m²); Image credits: "Rural Family Portrait" by Camilla Holmgren, "Village House Drawing" by Wang Cong; This article was expanded from its original publication as "Two Projects for Chinese Villages" in *Le Journal Spéciale Z*, edited by Sony Devabhaktuni

Jintai Village

Text: John Lin; Design: John Lin; Landscape Design:

Dorothy Tang; Project team: Crystal Kwan (Leader), Chan Yin Lun, Maxime Decaudin, Ashley Hinchcliffe, Huang Zhiyun, Ip Sin Ying, Jiang Meng; Project details: April 2012–ongoing / 4,000 m² / 4,800,000 RMB (600,000 USD) / 1,200 RMB/m² (150 USD/m²)

Changliu Village

Text: John Lin; Design: John Lin; Project team: Crystal Kwan (Leader), Ashley Hinchcliffe, Huang Zhiyun Project details: Oct 2011– ongoing / 15,400 m² (110 houses) / 15,400,000 RMB (2,510,000 USD) / 1,000 RMB/m² (160 USD/m²); This article was expanded from its original publication as "Two Projects for Chinese Villages" in *Le Journal Spéciale Z*, edited by Sony Devabhaktuni

All project details are listed in the following order: Date / Size / Cost / Unit Cost

---

Rural Urban Framework
Joshua Bolchover
and John Lin

The Department of Architecture
The University of Hong Kong
4/F Knowles Building
Pokfulam Road
Hong Kong

www.rufwork.org

IMPRINT

A CIP catalogue record for this book is available from the Library of Congress, Washington, DC, USA.

Bibliographic information published by the German National Library. The German National Library lists this publication in the Deutsche Nationalbibliografie; detailed bibliographic data are available on the Internet at http://dnb.dnb.de.

Birkhäuser Verlag GmbH
P. O. Box 44 | 4009 Basel
Switzerland
Part of De Gruyter

Printed on acid-free paper produced from chlorine-free pulp. TCF ∞

Printed in Germany
ISBN 978-3-03821-449-6

9 8 7 6 5 4 3 2 1
www.birkhauser.com